A904

Murgatroyd Started It!

Murgatroyd Started It!

Baroness Elizabeth Beck

COUNTRY LIFE LIMITED
LONDON

To the R.S.P.C.A., whose wonderful work I admire, and some of whose rescued animals feature in this book. Also to my husband Rolf, who is tolerant enough to let me keep all my animals.

First published in 1964
by Country Life Limited
2–10 Tavistock Street London WC2
Printed in Great Britain at
the Pitman Press,
Bath

Foreword

By JOY ADAMSON of Kenya

Liz Beck and I first met at a party in Suffolk in 1963. I was then at the end of a long lecture tour to raise funds for the conservation of wild life in Kenya. It was the coldest day of the coldest winter in thirty-five years, but the howling blizzard outside seemed only to stimulate the stories of the guests—all devoted animal lovers.

Liz and I felt from the first moment a great 'rapport' and so it seemed natural that she should respond to my invitation to come to Kenya to see the animals. On our safari, which took us to several of the East African Game Reserves and National Parks, we saw many varieties of wild animals. We discussed the question of keeping some of the smaller ones as pets. There is hardly any animal which is not irresistible when young, but few people really seem to understand the instincts of their pets. Any animal finds it difficult to adjust itself to changing owners, particularly if it has to change the place where it lives, since the territorial instinct is one of the strongest in any creature.

We also discussed the diet of animals in captivity and their need for companionship.

Liz Beck is certainly concerned about these problems and her book provides plenty of evidence that she understands the animals which she keeps. She not only writes brilliantly, but conveys in her writing her deep love and compassion for animals. Her book held me captive from beginning to end as I read the stories of her different animals, ending up with Bear. They are indeed a very varied menagerie for one person to have coped with!

Liz has the gift of making us share her feelings—and her book has the reader deeply moved at one minute and laughing hilariously at the next.

5

My own experience with wild animals in Africa has long convinced me that thought transference (which we humans may also have possessed before we developed speech) is a vital form of communication between animals. Has Bear contributed a new aspect to extra-sensory perception? We know so little yet about what motivates animal habits, but what we have learned within the last thirty years should make us—members of the genus *Homo sapiens*—very humble.

The author has not only provided us, in her book, with much amusement and new information about animals, but will certainly bring home to us all the responsibilities we have towards them.

Although she has a very busy life, Liz Beck has become an enthusiastic ally in our efforts to try to save wild animals and is now an active member and Trustee of the Elsa Wild Animal Appeal, a charitable organisation which is concerned with the conservation of wild life in Kenya.

I can only hope that, through the combined efforts of all of us who love animals, we will succeed in interesting others; and Liz has certainly made a great step towards this goal with her book. I wish it and her every success.

Contents

Illustrations

Acknowledgment

I would like to thank the following for kindly allowing me to use their photographs in this book: Ida Kar and the Editor of *Animals* magazine, Alan Robertson, John Simmons, Gordon Fairley of *Country Life*, Robert Chandler and the Editor of *The News of the World* and my friend Mr Bacon of Hadleigh.

1

Early Days

It is difficult to say exactly when it began, or why, but I seem always to have had the strangest animals. However, apart from one or two minor excursions into pet-keeping as a child, Murgatroyd started it. He was a fat white bouncing little gentleman, whom I really adored. The minor excursions prior to his arrival were really nothing very much to me, but I do remember that when I was about ten years old I was absolutely dotty about the scruffiest Rhode Island hen called Sally. For some reason that memory refuses to divulge, my father was determined to eat her, but he was out of luck. Sally lived long and dustily, finally earning her niche in this book by sitting on a tiny orphan black kitten I had rescued somewhere, rearing it devotedly, and setting the pattern, no doubt, for my endless mixing of quite improbable animals.

There was also General Sir Joseph Lynedoch. He was a vast Chinchilla rabbit, named after an august soldier, and unless he was under the schoolroom table I refused, quite rightly, to begin my lessons. He seemed to live to an immense age, and travelled everywhere with us. I remember he was remarkably stupid, and that after some years his 'wife' turned out to be just another bouncing buck.

At the age of fourteen I became possessed, in some way, of my first hooded white rat. I have another with me now, and still think that of all small pet animals they are the most charming, faithful, affectionate and intelligent. This one was called Angelica, and she lived and travelled in a cage tastefully covered in red flannel, with her name stitched across it. Had I been as dishonest then as I am now, she would have made a perfect foil in the Customs. Customs men of all nationalities were besotted with her, especially when she sat up on their dirty bleak boards, washing herself furiously all over with her delicate little pink hands. What they did not know, however, was that this was a sign of profound disgust that they had dared to touch her.

I remember that my mother and I went to stay in a beautiful convent in Bruges, with an exquisite marble staircase, that had once been the palace of Mary of Burgundy. In the fullness of time, of course, Angelica was discovered, and we were hauled before the Reverend Mother. Clearly, as if it were yesterday, I can see her grave face, as beautiful as the marble staircase, as she looked thoughtfully at the small offending animal. With the slightest smile she stretched out a thin hand to take her from me and, turning to the bustling, red-faced Sister, said gently: 'These also are God's children.'

Only recently I had a letter from my long-suffering governess of those days, who must now be nearly eighty, saying: 'Do you remember the year we went to France and took Angelica the white rat with us, and one day, by accident, I shut her tail in the bedroom door?' Oddly enough I don't, but if I listen hard enough I shall no doubt hear ghostly squeaks. Angelica died in France, in another convent, probably aged about three, which is the usual tiny life-span of these creatures. I remember the burial and the black despair. How things could hurt in those days!

However, to revert to Murgatroyd. Soon after I was married he could be seen frisking about our lawn, uttering festive cries. He was a middling large tame ferret, who had just been dumped on me for a 'good home.' He was, in fact, the first of the endless line of unwanted, unloved and deserted creatures that have since come my way. Except that in this case he was certainly not unloved.

He had belonged to a charming young man who, having to go abroad, had searched desperately for someone who could also love a ferret. And he had found one. But what Murgatroyd did not know, as he gambolled blissfully about his new home, was that Bonzo, my wonderful lurcher, had, only the day before, in a fit of jealousy, broken the back of a ferret I had just acquired. He left no mark, but it was a strange thing for a gypsy-trained dog to kill, though he had done it neatly and deliberately, and I was still very angry with him.

'Pouf!' said Murgatroyd, blowing out his white tail, and waltzing happily under the hard dark eyes of the watching dog. I watched too, but Murgatroyd didn't give a fig for all this nonsense, and his complete self-confidence seemed to awe Bonzo, who blinked rather sheepishly and wandered off. Now I was full of impatience to get started. I hadn't the faintest idea of how one set about ferreting, but scooping up my cheerful bundle, I called to the disgruntled dog and off we went.

When we got to a fairly large burry, I put Murgatroyd rather tentatively on the ground. Delighted, he bustled off and disappeared down a hole. I was distinctly alarmed, because there were a great many holes and there didn't seem any particular reason why he should return to me at all. I began thinking of all the things I should have done; vague memories of things heard, such as putting a ferret on a line and paying it out, rather like letting a bucket down a well, or fixing nets to tangle up him and the rabbit when they emerged. And spades. Yes, spades seemed definitely to play a large part in the game of ferreting.

Bonzo was looking puzzled too. I don't think he had ever been ferreting before either, so for once he was no good to me at all. Suddenly there was a quick hollow thumping underground and out shot a rabbit on the far side of the burry. Bonzo was utterly startled and it was a split second before he was off. It was a good course, but he was a better dog, and was soon cantering back. Scarcely had he put his prize into my hands when there was another wild thudding and off he went again. However, that seemed to be all, for after some moments out came Murgatroyd's white head and, stretching up to the full length of his ridiculous little neck, he peered around as though to say 'See? Pretty clever, aren't I—what?'

Gurgling with delight I gathered him up and stroked his funny little flat head. He had some mud on his nose and some stuck to his fore-paws, so I tried to clean him up a bit. He thought this was silly, and squeaked with annoyance, glaring at me out of his round red eyes. I stood corrected, and lifting him on to my shoulder again led off for another burry. We returned with four rabbits that evening, and by the sleepy contented look of him I knew that Bonzo had accepted Murgatroyd, if not as a chum, at any rate as a partner.

And what a partnership this was to prove! In our best season we accounted for just under three hundred rabbits, and this without nets or guns, or any sound other than underground thumping and the swift rush of a dog's feet over the grass.

But I doubt if I could do it again now, even given the skilled animals, and even though rabbits are definitely returning. With age has come a deep horror of taking life, and a much more painful realisation of the dreadful power of human beings over animals. And a more painful realisation still of how very little mercy human beings have. With Robert Burns:

> I'm truly sorry Man's dominion
> Has broken Nature's social union,
> An' justifies th' ill opinion
>   Which makes thee startle
> At me, thy poor, earth-born companion
>   An' fellow-mortal!

I wish I had known Robbie Burns; as an American might say: 'We should have gotten along just fine.'

No, I don't think I could do it again, although if rabbits have to be killed, surely it is the quickest and most merciful way; a skitter over the grass, a moment in a mouth soft as a gundog's, and one sharp blow behind the ears. I was always surprised that no rabbit ever struggled in Bonzo's mouth, nor when I took the inert feet for the kill. In the same way I have been vastly surprised that wild animals, the hunter and the hunted, live happily side by side, until the former feels the definite need of a meal. These are nature's laws, no doubt, and let us hope a measure of excuse for my young and quite impersonal brutality.

But all ferreting, of course, is not as kind as mine was. For

some strange reason, which I still cannot understand, ferrets
are fed on a horrible slop of bread and milk and starved before
they work. This produces the fairly obvious result that, being
meat eaters, and ravenous at that, the first rabbit they can drive
into an underground corner, they proceed to eat alive. They
start with the eyes, and the whole thing is quite unthinkable.
Then, gorged, they curl up and go to sleep, while angry sweating
men overhead are grappling with those famous spades.

But I can say, in perfect faith, that in the whole four years I
worked him Murgatroyd never killed and never once lay up—
I should have been properly perplexed if he had. But why should
he indeed? I knew nothing of this starving business and fed
him extremely well—cooked meat, scrambled egg, mashed
potatoes, and cake. I should think it just as sensible to starve
my labrador before taking him to pick up pheasants. My
simple brain works out that a starving dog might easily make a
quick meal of a bird. Both dog and ferret do their job instinc-
tively and for the fun of the thing, and the fitter they are the
more they enjoy it. I don't say they should have a heavy meal
before going out, but neither do I drink a pint of beer with my
lunch if I want to work.

With Murgatroyd, when I was tired of waiting by a large
burry, round which he was bustling—sometimes they were so
big that the rabbits just ran back and forth and were not much
bothered by a single ferret—I would rattle a stick in the mouth
of one or two holes and in a few seconds out he would pop,
looking round blindly and anxiously for me, as he had no
intention of being left behind. In fine weather he travelled on
my shoulder, in spite of the local farmer's insistence that one
day he would 'bite into you'm ear', and in wet weather he
travelled in my pocket.

Every Sunday morning Murgatroyd was given a thorough
bath in soapy water, for there is no denying that ferrets smell;
and he spent the day in the house. He made a great fuss about
having his bath, squeaking and spluttering furiously, but he
was delighted with the result, puffing out his clean tail and
emitting funny high-pitched little noises of pure pleasure. As I

watched him I thought of those other poor, half-starved ferrets
in their dirty dark cages, with their dreary bowls of bread and
milk, and the rough hands that stuffed them into old sacks to
take them out to work, and then pushed them down strange
holes. Why should they return to that—why should they not lie
up?

Murgatroyd made the very most of his day indoors, startling
guests by scooting out from under the furniture, plaguing the
dogs, and finishing up on my husband's lap, when he had
nodded off for his Sunday afternoon snooze. Invariably, upon
waking, my husband would fly into a rage and, seizing the
sleeping animal, would fling it across the room shouting
'Bloody ferret!' This only made me rock with laughter and made
Murgatroyd dance an extra jig. When Murgatroyd decided
there was no more fun to be had in that direction, he would curl
up in a ball between Bonzo's sleeping legs.

Bonzo was a remarkable dog. He had been bought from a
gypsy in Wales by a rather vague friend of mine who didn't
really want him, and asked, equally vaguely, did I? Did I!

Bonzo was completely poacher trained, and although I don't
suppose he showed me half of all he knew, he still showed me
a vast amount. For instance, he would slip through a fence,
and drift down, silent as a shadow. It was my job to know the
exact place that he stopped; to take two paces forward and
kick the fence sharply. In all cases, the rabbit would jump
straight into the waiting shadow's mouth. Then I had to watch
the fence again, and presently the slightest rustle would indicate
that Bonzo's head, with the rabbit, feet forward, was coming
through. I would take the rabbit without a word, and we would
continue on down. On one occasion we took five rabbits from
a short fence in this stealthy way. When the exercise was over
he would jump up on me, feathering his tail and showing his
teeth in a happy grin. We could make a noise then, and talk
and tell each other that we were all right, Jack, anyway according to ourselves.

Another ruse was equally successful. In the evening, when
the rabbits came out to feed, he would leave me, slink down a

Bonzo, who made a first-class rabbit-hunting team with
Murgatroyd.

Hard-boiled eggs are a great favourite with hooded white rats.

One of the many
pekingeses which the
author has owned.

Norah sleeping.

fence and drop into a ditch; then working his way along on his belly, would get between the feeding rabbits and their holes. When I appeared, there would be a general stampede and Bonzo would canter casually back with a rabbit limp in his mouth.

He had one poacher trick that was really a little unnerving. If we were walking along the road he would always stay closely to heel—until we met someone! Then he would disappear, doing a complete Cheshire cat act, because I never actually saw him go, and so far as the approaching person was concerned I had no dog. Some moments after the footsteps had died away, I would find him re-attached to my heels.

It was many years before he convinced himself that I was legal, and by that time I don't think he really minded any more. He was one of the greatest dogs I have ever owned. I adored him, and when he died of old age, he left a gap that would have been well nigh unbearable had something even more unbearable not happened along—the Second World War.

2

War Days

One of the most infuriating aspects of war, from my point of view, was the complete break-up of my animal world. Bonzo and Murgatroyd had gone to their chosen Heavens, but my poor horses had to be put down, and I was left tagging around with an enormous yellow dog, half alsatian, half samoyed, who was sweet and clumsy and faithful, but none too safe with strangers, and one whole problem to feed.

Lukie and I finally got to Fighter Command together, where extremely kind cousins took us in, but when I went to Officer Training, I had to have the big dog put to sleep. Poor Lukie.

Before I got to the stage of saluting women dressed up in uniforms or struggling with that dreadful calculation called 'co-ordinates', I spent quite a sizeable chunk of my own personal war filling shells and minding not to drop war-heads. I finally ended up with a commission in Intelligence in the Air Ministry, an event which my less kind friends suggest was entirely responsible for the undue length of the war. Be that as it may, I laboured for ten hours a day underground, and for the first time in my knowing life had no animal to care for.

I often thought back to the days of Angelica, but instead of hunting for a white rat, all I did about it was to sit gloomily watching the big sabre-toothed grey ones that galloped along the filthy pipes that adorned our concrete prison. In any case, by the time they were really active at night, I was so tired that I wasn't even sure that they were rats.

At the time I was a widow and sharing a flat with my mother. She was working strange hours at the India Office, and as we wrote notes to each other in this wonderful coming-and-going life, there wasn't much time to discuss or bemoan the lack of animals. But so far as I was concerned something had to give, and in the end, after many brief discussions, my mother agreed to help me look after a dachshund puppy. Dachshund, because it was small and short-coated and needed very little exercise and didn't eat much. Albeit unwillingly, she thought we might manage that.

So on my next day off (I think it had a more military term, but I have fortunately forgotten it) in high excitement I trotted up Bond Street and into a well-known dog shop. I drew a deep breath as I looked around at the anxious puppy faces—it seemed so long since I had had an animal! An obliging, if not unduly intelligent, young lady put an armful of wriggling dachshund puppies on the floor—black, golden tan, tan and black. They were all very sweet, but somehow I didn't feel quite with them. I had never had a dachshund before and, truth to tell, I hadn't really wanted one. But in the mood I was in that day I would have taken a starving goldfish and been thankful.

Just as I was trying to sort them out, the assistant dived into a cage and, dumping a fluffy puppy on the ground, reached to the back for yet another dachshund. The fluffy puppy shook itself, cocked a pale plume over its back, and swaggered to a long mirror on the wall. Here it sat up and admired itself in the glass. It had a black, black muzzle, bulging eyes, and a great deal of beautiful coat. I caught one huge dark eye in the mirror and the dark muzzle said a soft 'woof'. Almost trembling I pointed to it. 'I'll have that!' I said idiotically. The assistant turned and looked at me sadly. 'That, Madam,' she explained kindly, 'is not a dachshund.' 'No,' I said weakly, 'I don't suppose it is.'

And thus, foolishly, was William acquired—one of the greatest pekes that ever lived.

The assistant, finally convinced that I meant it, agreed to take my money, and we packed the strong chunky puppy into a wicker basket. As I was due for fire-watching, or some other tedious chore, that night and my mother would not be due back for half an hour, I left a rather nervous note on top of the basket and fled. Nervous, for there had been a definite embargo on a pekingese because of its long coat, determined character, and fussy eating habits. But when I got back next morning, all was well, of course. My mother already adored him.

To say that from then on, William was the light of my life, is a horrid cliché, but it happens to be true. After a trying day in those unpleasant cellars, when my boss, whom I loved dearly, but fought incessantly, had been particularly fractious, it was wonderful to know that, waiting behind the solid mahogany door of our flat, nose glued to the crack, there was a gay bouncing puppy with eyes already full of love. It made life bearable. How much he could give me, he who had nothing at all!

The war ground on, and presently I found myself engaged to be married. When I showed William to my husband-to-be, he enquired his age. Delighted by this show of interest from a definite non-dog man, I told him, only to be greeted by an agonised cry of 'What an awful long time he will live!' Partly because of this, and partly because I thought my mother would be lonely when I left her, after much selfish indecision I gave William to her. But I had a lesson here to learn. No doubt you can successfully, if heart-rendingly, give away other dogs, but not a pekingese. Day after day William lay, nose glued to that same door, until my mother could stand it no longer. She wrote, telling me to fetch him, and as we drove him away with us to the country, it would be nice to say that William was not looking smug. Nice, but quite untrue.

How he loved being in the country—how all pekes do! From that day on I'm afraid there was very little brushing and combing and he looked a proper rascal. In keeping with his looks, he fell madly and for all time in love with a huge and hideous mongrel sheep dog, who lived a good four miles away. At regular intervals he would plod the four miles to his lady love, and remain away for the night. One day, when we were driving home, we met him, very near her home. Of course, he recognised the car even before my cheerful shouts, but he looked the other way firmly and trudged ahead. When I seized his solid muddy body, he turned and looked at me in silent and conclusive fury. Of course, he escaped again that night and had those four miles

Norah loved and trusted the dogs.

Smaller than me, but rather alike in some ways.

Pups, Wallaby and the author's knee!

to do once again, so I rather saw his point. Therefore I took pains to find him a mate and we finally presented him with a delicious little pekingese bride called Honey. On first sight, he jumped onto the highest chair he could find and glared down savagely at her.

Where William was exceptional and why he comes into this story was because of his remarkable prowess as a gundog. I used to shoot in those days, before killing things so disgusted me that I gave it up, and when we went shooting, William, of course, came too. I spent endless time training my yellow labrador, but naturally paid little attention to a pekingese. So William's method, when evolved, was all his own.

He would take his place beside me, watching the sky in fervid concentration, and when a bird was hit he knew it instantly, and off he would go on those short stout legs of his, often arriving just as the bird hit the ground. It is no joke to say that in this way he saved us a lot of trouble looking for a runner, because, despite the enormous strength of a wounded cock pheasant, he never let one go.

With a dead bird, given time, he would drag it to me, or at least to within some feet of me, when there would start a silent battle of wits as to the rightful ownership of the bird. Finally William would give in, and spitting out a mouthful of feathers, would take his place again beside me, and resume his passionate study of the sky.

For some seasons we had the wonderful but expensive Brocket shoot, and in order to make it a financial proposition we let out some of the guns. The first day we gathered to meet our new chums it was a beautiful frosty morning, but honesty compels me to record that all the frost was certainly not on the ground. A woman with a gun is not 'top pops' with the serious shooting man, and if that woman has a pekingese attached to her, the insult is complete. There were sour smiles, and averted eyes, and obvious fury at parting with so much money to join in such a circus. The only perfectly happy members of that party were my husband, who was quite unaware of the frigid atmosphere, and William, who was studying the newcomers with patronising interest. However, three seasons later William was so much part of that shoot that all were concerned if he did not come out, and, as he grew older, the keepers automatically picked him up and toted him over very rough ground. He was the devil of a weight, but they were really fond of him by then. I once saw Lord Wimborne most good-humouredly disputing the ownership of a partridge with William, though there was not the slightest doubt as to the outcome of that issue. William could carry a partridge, and, wearing this particular one like a moustache across his flat face, he trotted it proudly over to me, and when I returned it to its rightful owner there was no need for apology.

When William was getting really old, nearly blind in one eye and almost deaf, we had to move to London. He didn't really mind then, and I was so glad he had had his wonderful seasons of shooting. One night my husband took him for a last run, and a taxi ran over him. Literally ran over him, as he seemed not to be touched in any way, and may have died of a heart attack. I simply couldn't believe it as I held the limp body on my lap, and I cried and cried. My husband, who had also grown to love William, did his best to comfort me, finally saying rather helplessly: 'I wonder if you would cry so much if I was run over.' To which I replied in bitter fury: 'I wish you'd go out and try, and then we'd be quite sure about it.' My poor husband has had his trying moments.

3

London Days

We still had Michael, a yellow labrador, and Hoolie, a perfectly sweet, if not very clever, pekingese. But if Hoolie was not clever, Michael was—among other things he was a brilliant gundog, who had only had my very amateur training—he was steady as a rock, fast, would swim or jump anything, and marked my birds better than I did. I had bred him, and although like many another good dog he was rather plain, I was extremely proud of him.

Although a country dog, he had settled into London life remarkably well, and never once went on a collar or lead. When I rode in the Row (where I should think I established a record by getting myself knocked out and ending up in the London Clinic) he came too. He would follow on from the stable, watching the lights, or I suppose, really, waiting for other people to cross, and once in the park he would always stay to one side of the track so that he did not get in the way of other horses. We still went shooting on Saturdays during the season, and he was as good as ever.

But ill-luck was after us again. Somehow, somewhere, in dirty London, we picked up that horrible disease, Hard Pad, about which very little was then known. A new serum was flown from Scotland, but to no avail. Poor little Hoolie died at once. Michael struggled bravely on, although his pads shrunk horribly, and became as hard as iron: the name Hard Pad was not coined just for the fun of it. We had an excellent vet attending him day and night, and I pushed horrid things down his patient throat, but finally he simply faded away, and a post-mortem showed that his liver had quite disintegrated. With the efficient inoculations of today so beastly a thing need never

23

happen, but there we were, with little Hoolie's pathetic harness hanging in the hall, and Michael's empty basket by my bed.

I passionately dislike living in London, but to be cooped up there without an animal of any sort was going beyond the limit. On the other hand, we escaped abroad as often as possible, and leaving the dogs behind was no fun for any one of us, either. The last time we had gone, Michael had rushed down-stairs with us, carrying his bone. The luggage was all stowed away, and understanding that he was not wanted, he sat down dejectedly. As we drove away, his bone dropped to the pave-ment, and it was one of the saddest sounds I have ever heard. Leaving grown house-trained dogs behind is possible: leaving a puppy is quite definitely not.

'Never mind,' I said to my son, who was then four years old and couldn't understand what on earth had happened to the dogs, 'I'll find us something.'

And then at last I thought back to Angelica. But thinking back alone was not much help, because fashions in animals change in an astonishing way, and I discovered that white rats had entirely disappeared. Mice I could have, and hamsters I could have, oh, any amount of hamsters, but not white rats.

'Why not rats?' I asked peevishly at the last pet shop on my list.

'No call for them, Madam,' was the mild reply.

'Nonsense,' I said rudely, 'you know perfectly well there's a "call" for whatever you choose to stock, and the hooded white rat is the best little animal a child can have.'

Finally, rather weakly, and because I couldn't face that animal-empty flat again, I was persuaded to buy a cream hamster, a pretty enough little chap for whom I paid a guinea. Thinking this really was quite fun after all, I hurried home and took him straight up to my little boy, Stephen. Steve was delighted. He had never seen a rat or mouse or hamster before, and the sparkling eyes and inquisitive twitching whiskers intrigued him greatly. A few seconds later he was a good deal less delighted, for the nasty little thing had bitten him right through one of his small fingers. Of course he yelled in pain and fright—who wouldn't—and while I was crooning motherly noises to him, the hamster skittered across the floor and disappeared down a hitherto unknown mousehole. So much for my guinea. And, as far as I am concerned, so much for hamsters altogether.

Frustrated and infuriated, I sat down to think again. Where, if no pet shop had them, would one find a white rat. Laboratories, I thought sourly. Hospitals was another idea. And then—Doctor! Of course, our doctor. Enchanted by the brilliance of this, I telephoned him at once. Only to be knocked flat again when a very nice male voice told me he was away.

'But I can get you another doctor,' it added helpfully.

'Well, as a matter of fact,' I said, feeling a perfect fool, 'it isn't a doctor I want, it's a white rat.'

'Oh,' said the voice, not in the least put out, 'I see. Well, that's different, isn't it?'

It certainly was. There was a pause, and then the voice came again.

'Why don't you try a firm called "Finders"? They're people who claim to find anything. Hold on a second and I'll get you the number.'

I never did find out who that voice belonged to, but I am forever in its debt. Still feeling rather foolish, I telephoned 'Finders'.

'I want a white rat,' I said doubtfully.

'White rat,' came the cheerful reply. 'Must you have it today?'

'Why, no,' I said, rather staggered. 'It's not really as urgent as all that. Can you find me one?'

'Oh yes,' came back airily. 'We'll ring you back and tell you where to collect it.'

And so they did. The next day I went to a Medical Research Centre to collect a tiny hooded white rat with little pink hands like Angelica. And throughout the years I have been going there at irregular intervals ever since.

When I brought him back to the flat (I had asked for a her, but what matter), Stephen was not going to be caught again and he was exceedingly cautious. Same wobbly whiskers, same bright eyes, but the little rat was gentleness itself. And how we enjoyed having him about the place. He lived in a tin-lined hamster cage on the landing (tin against hamsters' vicious little teeth) but it was never closed, and Rattle Pratt, as he came to be, magnanimously ignored the tin. He used to gallop about the landing and into my room, but he never went downstairs. He used to sleep most of the day, but when I came up around five o'clock, he used to rush out to see what there was to eat. Rats can survive on almost anything, but, of course, they have their preferences, and egg in any shape takes top place. We used to have fun putting the food quite a long way off, and watching him pick it up piece by piece and gallop it back to his box. Rats pace themselves with food and never over eat, so to avoid a lot of stale stuff lying about, we had to be rather careful of the amount we gave him. He loved chocolate, and lettuce, and cake, and chicken, but not meat very much, and cheese not at all. He was utterly gentle, never attempted to bite, and as for running away, his only idea of bliss was to be with us as much as possible: on our laps, in our beds, in our pockets. I never have been able to understand this absolute faith and trust that white rats put in human beings, but there it is, and I am grateful for it.

Whenever we went abroad, Rattle came too. He travelled in a tennis ball box, and spent the day in a drawer or cupboard, and as he slept most of the time, I imagine that he was never found in hotels—at least we had no complaints.

One day in Constantinople, or less romantically Istanbul, some business associates of my husband came to pay a call. It was getting on towards evening and they came up to our suite for a drink in that American home from home, the Hilton Hotel. I wasn't thinking of anything in particular when suddenly our guests let out a frantic yell, and I saw that Rattle Pratt had wobbled rather sleepily into the room, and was peering around to choose a lap upon which to establish himself. My husband, who had not seen him, was surprised by this rather noisy interruption from the Turks, but I realised at once that they thought he was a wild rat, and scooping him up with muffled laughter, I removed him back to the bathroom. Somehow business didn't seem to go so well after that, and I was rather sorry for the Turks, who probably saw a lot more of rats than they could really enjoy.

Feeding Rattle on his journeys was rather a comic turn too. I used to slip small bits of hard boiled egg and chicken and lettuce, and the odd bean into my bag, and people who saw me can only have thought me potty—the mad English indeed—or maybe they thought me a martyr to night starvation. But none of that mattered when Rattle rushed out of his drawer to see what I had filched for him, seizing everything gratefully in his tiny hands and whisking back to his temporary home.

4

Back to the Country

We now felt that life in London was intolerable, and since we had a little more money, we decided to move into the country again. But the great question was—where? Being from the West Country my own counties were too far away, and yet I hated the thought of the Home Counties—they seem to me nowadays to be neither one thing nor the other. Also the idea of breaking into any new county without a trial run is pretty chilling—you may not like the people, but a much more horrible thought is that the people may not like you.

Then one day my mother rang up to say that there was a Suffolk manor house advertised in *The Times* (a paper which we did not at that time take). The house was to let, for one year or two, furnished, while the owner was abroad. We duly trundled down, liked what we saw, and negotiated to rent it. The owner came back, briefly, from Paris, where he was stationed, for being a pretty thorough sort of man, he thought he had better have a look at me, from the 'suitable tenant' point of view.

So it was arranged that he should come to tea at our flat in Chesham Place. Although we had had a hard financial struggle we still had some pretty and decorative possessions; and the flat had a beautiful drawing room with an open fireplace, that almost made living in London tolerable. Almost, but not quite.

The Major duly arrived. He was charming and good-looking, and I behaved just beautifully for once. After a while, and a good look round the flat, I could tell he thought me quite reasonable material for a tenancy of his home (artistic, orderly, good housewife, and all that jazz) and we spent a very enjoyable tea-time together. Just as he was leaving, when I hoped it was too late for him to back down, I dropped my bombshell.

28

Fricky (the Thick-Tailed Bush-Baby) stares wide-eyed at the light.

Our experiments to bring Fricky and Infestus together finally met with success.

Two owls, at one time members of the author's animal family.

'I hope you won't mind if I bring my white rat with me,' I said, in a casual tone.

'White rat!' he repeated, obviously quite dumbfounded.

'Yes,' I said brightly. 'Chinese hooded white rat, you know' (which quite clearly he didn't). 'They're the sweetest little animals and very well behaved. She won't do any harm to your house, I promise.' This was too much for the poor Major, used to dealing with military problems, so after stuttering a bit, he gave in quite gracefully. Nowadays we are near neighbours and close friends, and we often laugh at our near-Victorian tea party and the sudden dreadful *dénouement* of the small white rat.

Rattle and I had a few more hoops to go through before we got down to happy Suffolk. One of the more trying was when I gaily blew off a piece of my arm when experimenting with a shot-gun. That put me in the great St Thomas's Hospital for close on three months. Most of this time I spent in Alexandra Ward, in the care of wonderful Barbara Tyler—Sister Alex to us—and when I was shunted, protesting, into a private room, Rattle arrived in a shoe box almost at once. To my great delight I was allowed to keep him, and he lived on the top shelf of the cupboard. I'm not sure whether they knew he slept in my bed all night, but I was so thrilled to have him again that I had no intention of leaving him way up on a silly shelf all by himself. The nurses adored him, spoiled him, and never stopped feeding him, because it was fascinating to watch him take whatever tit-bit it might be in his delicate little pink hands, sit up on his haunches and eat it carefully and cleanly, finishing up with a good wash of his face, hands and ears.

We spent a happy year and a half on the Major's Suffolk estate, and ended up by buying our own house some five miles away. We have since acquired a good bit of land around the house, and as the house stands well back from the road, this now allows me to keep all the strange animals that come my way. Well, when I say 'come my way' this is not strictly true. I precipitate their arrival in many cases. It was entirely my doing that Norah came to our home.

5

'Norah'

George Orwell's rating of the intelligence of a pig in his book, *Animal Farm*, had always impressed me deeply. For years, stored in the back of my mind was the determination to try to keep one as a pet. So one day, walking round a friend's farm to admire the litters of tiny pink pigs, I quite suddenly, and surprisingly, asked if I might have one. Our host was certainly startled, but being also very kind, he shrugged his shoulders and told me to take my pick. His astonished stockman selected a nice, four square animal and set it before me. 'This one is about the best' he muttered, looking a little dazed. But I had spotted a small thing shivering in the background, apart, independent, and with a knowing look in her eye. I pointed. The stockman, looking quite resigned, stuffed her into an old cardboard box, and into the back of our car. As we drove away my husband said to me quietly, without rancour, but somewhat bitterly I thought: 'You are entirely mad.' I only laughed: we'd see. (Me and George Orwell, that was!)

From the moment we arrived home, this tiny silky pig established herself as a 'character'. She was impatient of the lamb's feeding teat which I had unearthed, knocking it crossly aside to drink out of the bowl. Then came my moment of doubt: would the dogs—labradors—with whom I intended her to live, accept her. I know that very occasionally animals will not mix, from the case of my cherished white rat. The dogs, with whom Ratty was so anxious to be friendly, couldn't stand the sight of him. So, with certain anxiety, the labradors were called in. Mother and daughter bounded into the drawing room, and their looks of astonishment were really very funny. They approached the little creature gingerly and sniffed her over, while she, for her part, inspected them from under her long white lashes. 'Humph!' she said. This seemed to delight the labradors— mother licked her, while daughter hastened to steal her milk.

It was odd how she at once placed their ages: Binnie became her adopted mother, and Itsy her inseparable companion; she followed Itsy everywhere, but always snoozed or slept against Binnie's comfortable bulk. And both the dogs adored her.

From the very first she trotted in and out with the dogs, lay with them by the fire, and shared their scraps of cake or biscuit. There was no nonsense about weaning her—she even managed, and greatly cared for, the tea-time lump of sugar. But there was one difference between her and the dogs: whereas the dogs are always rather messy about eating, she was an absolute vacuum cleaner—with her round cushion of a nose exactly angled, she left the carpet spotless.

Anyone who has house-trained a puppy knows the devil it can be. Puddle, puddle, puddle, wallop, wallop, wallop. I had just finished with Itsy, and now here was Norah. But for a surprisingly long time nothing happened. Then one day I watched her back carefully up to the skirting board in the sitting room, and there leave a puddle. I fell upon her. It's a funny sensation smacking a pig, but smack her I did, and the resultant rage was comical. Whereas a dog will cringe, look puzzled or even aloof, there was not the shadow of a doubt about it, Norah was downright mad. Stiffening her ludicrous little legs she bounced up and down, squeaking and grunting at the same time—squeak-in, grunt-out—and wagging her head up and down like an infuriated mandarin. I picked her up, and to this variation of the bagpipes carried her on to the lawn. It is hard to credit, but she never did make a mistake in the sitting room again. Quite a little while later we had a similar contretemps in the dining room, but here she was less vehement—it was almost as though she said to herself 'Oh Lord—it's obvious this is forbidden territory, too'. But her third and last attempt was quite another matter.

She was accustomed now to trot daintily over the parquet with her neat white shoes, to use the carpets very suitably for relaxation, and not to put a foot wrong; which was just as well as every guest wanted to see this phenomenon-about-the-house. But one day she discovered the stone hearth in my husband's study. There are many other, but entirely different stone hearths about the house. This one obviously has a strangely 'corner-of-the-cowshed' look to it. Norah distinctly approved. She may have been there before for all I know, but one day I saw her purposefully trot across the drawing room, and wriggle round the door. I followed. I found the tiny figure backed modestly into the corner of the hearth place, lashes demurely lowered. It was a position I fully understood, and retribution was swift.

After the first squeal of astonishment a sense of outraged injustice and fury overcame her. She was obeying my rules wasn't she, not sullying my stupid old parquet or carpets, wiping her feet on the mat almost, and here she'd found a nice old stone bit of out-of-doors, and that wouldn't do either. Really it was too bad. Here the screams turned to a rending lament, and something unbelievably like sobbing. Unmoved, I dumped her on the lawn. The noise stopped abruptly, and with a furious swish of the, as yet, uncurled tail, a very angry little pig indeed took herself off to sulk.

As I have said, whenever there were guests, in Norah had to come. We would hear her soft exploratory little grunt as she came across the hall (the squeak-in, grunt-out was only when she was upset). And she became very like a prima-donna about these appearances. To encourage her public she would toss her head about, swizzle that ridiculous tail, and execute foolish little dances. There was never any coffee sugar left when she was finally removed, but where a dog would look eagerly for it, and wag a tail in appreciation, Norah never said 'please', and only a brief 'thank you'. She was a most dignified little animal: what you gave her she was very pleased to accept daintily and cleanly, but she was quite happy just to be around. Eat like a pig indeed. I was becoming very Orwellian.

Norah was charming in the house, but she was just as amusing outside. Given the chance she would trot after Itsy all day,

Jão (the sad!) holding one of his charges. At the time of this picture he had already sustained many bites during his lifetime with snakes.

One of the snake pits, with flowering trees and circular terra-cotta shelters for the snakes.

'A charming model.' A False Coral Snake which was given to the author and ultimately returned to the snake farm, since it required to be fed on live mice!

steadily and devotedly, eye-lashes lowered—then suddenly an 'interesting to a pig smell' would take her keen fancy, and explore it she must. She would inspect it minutely, until suddenly she realised that the blond hairy legs that had been trotting before her a moment ago had vanished. With a shriek like a train whistle she would be off, showing astonishing speed and grunting wildly. 'Humph humph' she would say, casually if breathlessly, as she regained her objective, and with a slight shrug of the backside, would dismiss her recent agitation to resume the patient plodding. But there was play as well as plodding. Anyone who has seen the furious exercise that two under-worked young labradors take to amuse themselves will appreciate that this tiny pig became just an unwanted football in the game. I know now that I should have taken her out of it, but at the time I did not realise how constitutionally delicate is the pig; and she simply loved the rough and tumble of it all, spending a lot of time circulating round the garden, getting in the way, falling over and being fallen over.

By this time she had her own apartments, and although there was very great excitement to come out, she was always happy to go back. On days when for some reason the labradors were shut up she would shift her devotion to me—indeed, I have never been followed so closely by any other animal. I found something very companionable about the soft grunt that followed me, and I had the strange feeling that she understood far more of what I was saying to her than did any of my dogs.

We have a good deal of ornamental water around the house, and this led to the legend being explained to me (by a countryman at that) that never must pigs attempt to swim: they cut their throats with their own front feet if they do. Frankly I gave it little thought. But one day when I was weeding some of the miles of rock-garden that run beside the pool, of course trailed by the labradors and Norah, something made me turn round. And it was indeed something! Across the pond steamed Norah, for all the world like an exercising submarine, the water rising well before her upcast snout. Dropping everything, and with a cry like a bereaved mother, I flew to the pond. Norah at that

moment was coming in to land. As I hauled her out she regarded me calmly from under the long white lashes and it was
one of several occasions when I fairly felt put in my place. As
I dried her, much to her satisfaction, on a large rough towel, I
thought: 'If Norah does nothing else she has at least blown one
stupid fable sky-high.' Pigs can swim, and extremely well at
that. After this she took to regular bathing in the shallow
streams, a favourite pastime with the dogs, lying contentedly
with them in the sun-warmed water.

Then one morning she was a little lame in the hind-quarters.
With all the junketing and bathing it really was small wonder,
and I was not unduly worried. But when I returned from a trip
the following weekend everyone had long faces: Norah could
no longer raise herself on her hind legs. Our vet was called. At
first we thought it might be cramp, and she had the appropriate
injections. It made her no better and no worse. I massaged her
back and rubbed in embrocation; the hind legs remained
obdurate. I harried anyone I knew who owned pigs, asking
advice, and comparing notes feverishly on any similar illness
that their animals might have had. I even dragged in our kind
doctor, who diagnosed paralysis, caused either by a blow or a
chill, and he thereupon had strange concoctions made up for
us, but her condition remained the same.

Norah was not in any pain, and she still took tremendous
enjoyment in what was left of her life, co-operating whole-
heartedly in front when I raised her hind-quarters in a sling.
This was, in fact, a terrible game, because by now she had
grown extremely heavy, and by the time I had trundled this
lively and unpredictable wheelbarrow round onto the lawn, I
was quite exhausted. But it amused her, and here she could sit on
some sacking, with a dog-coat over her loins, enjoying the sun
and watching all that went on. One could see now how fond of
her were the dogs, because they would always lie with her
between their games and forbidden hunting, much to her joy;
but when they inevitably went off again, it was pathetic to see
her hopeful efforts to follow; the small front feet would beat the
ground uselessly, and the grunting rise to a disappointed squeak.

At last I began to fear there was no hope. And one day when I went round to her box, she could scarcely raise her head. She lay there with her eyes half closed, breathing painfully, and I knew she had pneumonia. It was the end. The vet was called, and there was nothing left for me to do but say a very tearful farewell. It was a moment of great sorrow.

Norah's life was all too short, but it was vastly happy, and I learnt a prodigious amount about a pig. Above all I was impressed by her cleanliness and great intelligence. And this, added to her fondness for people, her gaiety, her comical temper, and tremendous love of fun, puts her very high on my list of favourite animals. I shall never forget her. I like to think that the briefness of her life was truly counterbalanced by its carefree happiness, and by the friendship she received from dogs and humans alike.

6

'Africa'

After the sad passing of Norah, there were just two labradors left, Pekie, and the wallaby which I had recently been given and for which we never really developed a great deal of affection. He lived in the house for some time and got quite tame, but when we put him out loose on the tennis court in the summer, he acquired a great timidity and we found him very difficult to catch. Finally we put him into a nice large moveable cage and he spent his life cropping lazily at the grass and plantains.

When he was 'about the house' he became quite friendly with Infestus, yet another white rat. We called this rat Infestus because my husband had exclaimed in exasperation 'Now you are going to infest us with white rats again', when I showed him the tiny, newly arrived replacement for poor dear Ratty. (The only, absolutely only, fault I can find with white rats as pets is their sadly short life span.)

These animals made a very adequate family, and I had no thought in mind to increase it, apart from the odd litter of labradors from time to time, to keep a continuity of gundogs. However, fate was creeping up on me again, and one day Steve and I found ourselves in a pet shop. I think them quite sickening places, but the fascination that animals have for me weakens my will, and I find it very hard to pass them by. Of course guinea pigs, rabbits, white rats, mice and kittens can make charming pets for children, and one hopes they do not suffer too much in the process; but to my way of thinking there should be an Act of Parliament forbidding the importation of wild animals except to really well-qualified and well-inspected zoos. This being the case, of course, I should not have had the fun and

Susie was never really keen on walking. Here she is sulking a little.

She nipped quickly into the baker's van and won this prize.

Contented, I sit in the sun.

the excitement of my wild animals, but neither should I have had to watch their bewilderment and suffering as they strove to adjust themselves to an alien way of life; nor to seek homes for the poor souls when they got too strong, or too discontented; and on the whole I think we should both have been far better off this way.

My first wild animal of all, who now pops his head up between these pages, was an exception to the rule. It was in this animal shop that we acquired him. That is to say, we stared at him as he clung miserably to the bars of his cage that had been put on the floor, while a bunch of unpleasant children kept poking him with something that looked like a chewed up pencil.

'Mummy,' said Steve, with his usual forthrightness, 'you can't leave him here.'

'But, darling,' I said uneasily, 'I don't even know what it is.'

'Well, you can ask,' replied my son, with perfect reason. It was, I was informed, a bush-baby, though it was not like any bush-baby I had ever seen. I looked at it rather helplessly. I didn't know where to keep it, how to look after it, I didn't want it, I couldn't afford it—and I left the shop with it. But at least I could put a little of the blame for this purchase on to Steve!

When we got back to the flat we let him out of the silly cumbersome travelling dog-kennel we had been bounced into buying for him. He seemed very dazed, as he crawled pathetically across the floor. I had noticed before, and I noticed again, the thick, coarse harness that had been strapped on to him, cutting into the delicate skin under his arms and rubbing a bare patch under his chin. Something made me feel that it had not been put on very kindly, and just as soon as I could unearth a sharp pair of scissors, with Stephen's help, I hacked it off. The queer creature stared at me with his very round, flat eyes. I picked him up to put him back in the dog-kennel, as we had to go out again, and said a loud 'Damn!' This was the first bite I had from him—the first of many, many hundreds. I was more surprised than hurt.

During the next few days, before going back to the country, I found out a little about the new member of our family. He was not the more usual bush-baby imported into this country, which is Galago Maholi, a little chap with pink hands and enormous eyes, such as I have at the moment. He was Galago Crassicaudatus, or the Thick-Tailed Bush-Baby, which is twice the size, has large black hands, small eyes by comparison, and as the name would suggest, when adult, a beautiful full thick tail. Galago means monkey, and the bush-baby is a Primate, so off I went to pay a visit to the Monkey House in Regent's Park. This was a bit abortive as the Head Keeper was not there, but I was sternly told that on no account could I put the bush-baby and my white rat together: one was a Primate, the other a Rodent, and never the twain should meet; it was by no means clear which was supposed to eat which, but the vista was altogether bloody. I also learnt, rather to my horror, that mealie worms were an essential part of a bush-baby's diet. Apparently, having achieved the beastly things, one kept them in a tin of bran, and they lasted quite a while. Steve and I finally ran some to earth in an animal shop in the wilds of Camden Town. They looked disgustingly like maggots.

One other thing I did in the cause of bush-baby-ship, and that was to buy George Cansdale's excellent book on how to keep and look after them. This was a good move, because without it I should have been entirely lost. On skimming through I found that Crassicaudatus was found south of the Sahara, so, thinking of his large black hands, I named him Africa, which promptly degenerated, alas, into Fricky-Pic.

So off we trundled to Suffolk, with the dreadful 'Pekingese Pagoda' kennel overhousing its tiny occupant. As it was winter I had wrapped him in a very soft woolly, and had covered the wire door with cardboard. Everyone had frightened me with regard to keeping him warm—in my innocence (or stupidity) I had even bought a thermometer so as to keep his temperature to an even 70 degrees, as this was the specified norm. Later, much later, when I was discovering many interesting things about him, I came to ask myself how I could have been so dim-witted as to imagine that any wild animal lived in a perfectly even temperature, day and night—indeed the climatic changes in the tropics are extremely startling, as well I know. But the voice of Animal Authority I have often found is as drastic as it is didactic—the pronouncement is made, and there is nothing further to discuss.

After I had had Fricky for some six months, I was able to look back in horror on the condition in which that poor little bush-baby came to me. The muscles of his hind legs were almost atrophied, those wonderful, powerful hind legs that give them a greater spring than anything twice their size. All he could then manage was to haul himself painfully up on to a not too high chair with his large black hands. I knew nothing of bush-babies then, but he seemed to me a pretty slow creature all the same. 'He's not even as active as Infestus,' I said to Steve in disgust. Had I but known what was in store for me when he regained his strength!

At first he was extremely savage, biting my hands and fingers repeatedly with his pin-like teeth; and I was depressed to read in George Cansdale's book that some bush-babies never will submit to being handled, even by their owners. Anyway for some months my hands were a most un-pretty sight; and although, in the end, he became one of my most adored animals, never would I recommend any bush-baby as a pet, and of all the genus, the Thick-Tailed least of all. Not for the biting— dear Fricky soon grew out of that—but because they have an unfortunate habit of urinating on their hands; and not only does this make all furniture stickier than a child with a lollipop, but the smell of it finally permeates everything, every place, with quite unmistakable monkey. I did get to wondering why he had this habit. I suppose the answer, really, is that they are marking out their territory—at least this seems to be the generally accepted reason—though in the back of my mind joggles the idea that, since their funny suction feet have no claws, maybe they do it to get a better grip at the end of their leaps, because I have noticed that they do it especially before they take off on one of their more startling round the house acts. Fricky at this time was a skinny, feeble and bad tempered little creature. He crawled about my bedroom and bathroom, sleeping in a shoe box in my cupboard most of the day and coming out hungry in the evening. The next thing was to find out what he really liked to eat—despite Authority's assurance, the mealie worms, thank goodness, revolted him, so I wasn't even going to trust to Mr Cansdale's book on this score. When I think back to Fricky now, it is to think that he was the first wild animal whose diet I had to discover the good old hard way, and since his happy day I have been doing much the same thing, off and on, for many other orphans.

Milk and bananas and mealie worms was the official diet. We evolved scrambled egg, lettuce, chocolate, Haliborange (and to hell with the temperature), Dundee cake and grapes as top favourites. And he liked his milk without anything floating in it. I loved to watch him picking up his food with his knobbly, knuckly black hands, egg in the one, lettuce in the other. He would sit up on his adequate rump, and fall to with abandon, though I cannot say that his table manners were very praise-worthy—when he had had enough of anything he just flung it on the floor and grabbed up the next course.

By this time his muscles were coming back into use and he hopped about like a kangaroo. He had not reached the flying leap stage yet, but I had long since realised that when he came to me, he had been in a very bad state. The biting was diminish-ing too, and I used to take him down to the Boudoir (my sitting room was christened that by the architect who altered the house!) in the evenings to hop around and play. There is a good deal of quite valuable china about the house, and particu-larly in a Suffolk corner cupboard in the Boudoir, but during all the time I had him he broke absolutely nothing. He could weave in and out of the plates and figures and bowls, to the utter consternation of any guests present, the consternation being mainly that they thought me mad.

No, he did absolutely no harm to the china, but never in my life have I cleaned so many acres of furniture as I did while Fricky was with me; and I would gladly clean ten times as much again if only I could bring him back to life.

By this time I was beginning to chafe at the embargo put on

a meeting between Fricky and Infestus. It meant that the door
between my bath and bedroom had to be glued shut when I
came up in the evening, with one animal kept one side and one
the other, as both were, of course, nocturnal. I asked Peter, who
is head animal man as well as head gardener, what he thought.
This was pretty silly of me, because after all, what could he
think in the face of stark, uncompromising statements that the
Rodent was utterly unacceptable to the Primate (and the other
way round!). Still, taking a look at his face I knew he was
suffering grave doubts too.

'If they did, which do you think would have a go at which?'
I asked him, which was an equally stupid question. So we did
nothing that day and the dreary segregation dragged on. But I
have always firmly believed that, as a general rule, if animals
are well-fed, secure and without any sex disturbance, there is no
reason why differing species should not get on together beautifully. The thing that has always shaken even me is the case of
Steve's beautiful hunting white cat. That cat since kittenhood
has pretty well fed itself on rats, mice, water rats, voles, and I
regret to say birds, when she can get them, and yet she pays no
attention at all to Infestus, and many a time she must have been
alone in a room with him, because I am hopeless at shutting
doors. Infestus roams and the white cat patrols the house.

I think it was this fact that finally made up my anxious mind.
Peter came up to my room with me to lend support, and we
opened the communicating doors. Fricky flew through to the
bedroom blissfully. But I suddenly lost my nerve and snatched
Infestus off the floor. Fricky leapt up the curtain and his light,
flat eyes took in the scene. Festie was sitting in my hands quiet
and happy—as much as most bush-babies dislike handling,
white rats adore it—and I started to weigh up their chances.
Fricky was nearly three times the size of Infestus, his clawless
hands were very powerful, and my own still swollen hands bore
witness to his teeth. On the other hand, stripping all sentiment
aside, Festie was a big buck rat in his prime, and I couldn't
exactly see him rolling over on his back to be chewed up. I
remembered with amusement the short while back when I had

given him a wife. He sniffed her once, seized her in his powerful jaws by the scruff of the neck, and disappeared into his cardboard box with her. After that he ignored her very existence, and his children bored him to sobs. No, I didn't somehow think he was defenceless, and I knew from his own placid gentleness that he would not be the first to attack. So I put him on the top of a small chest of drawers. Fricky watched unblinking from the top of the pelmet board. Festie ran lightly along the chest of drawers, looking for a way down. And suddenly Fricky leapt.

'Oh Peter! Do you think it's all right?' I gasped, sticking my fist into my mouth in best dramatic style, as Fricky, in two bounds, was up on the chest of drawers, and had pounced on Festie. I think Peter and I were both frozen to the floor. But it didn't seem to bother Infestus one wit. He shook off the black rubber hand that was gripping his ear and toddled again to the edge of the chest of drawers—white rats have an extraordinary one track mind and Infestus was bent on getting down to come in search of me. Fricky looked doubtfully at the fat white behind with its stiff tail in balance, teetering on the edge of the chest of drawers. He approached gingerly, and gave a tentative sniff, and then with a sudden wild, typically bush-baby leap, he was off again round the room.

'Whew!' said Peter and I simultaneously. My relief was boundless, because I knew that finally they were certain to get together, because if my life depended on it I could not be depended upon to close a door behind me.

Infestus lived in a cardboard box with a hole in it in the corner of my bathroom. In a corner of it he kept his store of food—rats are very careful housekeepers. After their memorable meeting, Africa the bush-baby was moved into the bathroom too, and there, theoretically, they should both have stayed, and would have, but for that fateful door. As it was, Fricky was usually to be found on top of my bedroom curtains after five o'clock in the evening, and Infestus probably in my bed. This caused an amusing incident. Some very well-known and very dear friends of mine were at a rather formal party, when she, in her charming, clear voice said: 'Eric *was* so surprised to find a rat in Liz's bed.' This dire discovery came about when both Eric and Infestus were visiting our London flat, and I knew jolly well where I should find Festie when I wanted to display him to Eric.

Now that all the nonsense about Primates and Rodents had been set at naught, there was the problem of transporting the assortment backwards and forwards to London. I had an old rectangular beauty case, an article of luggage that none of we girls feel 'travel-dressed' without. One day when I had to be up in Town rather longer than usual, I punched several holes in this case, lined it with a woolly, and, while Fricky slept, I planted him therein. Then, after some hesitation (but not much) I popped the almost equally sleepy Infestus in on top of him and gently closed the lid. 'Well,' I thought to myself, as no sounds emerged, 'let's hope Authority goes on being wrong, that's all.'

Some hours later, when we reached London and I peeped inside their box I was astonished to see Infestus clasped in Fricky Pic's arms, and his head tucked in below the cosy woolly chin. 'Well!' I thought, 'what a perfect hot water bottle for Fricky. No worry about travel temperature now.' And from that time onwards they always travelled like that. Like all animals (and babies) I think they enjoyed the rocking of trains and cars and boats, and air travel worried them not at all.

Fricky was very happy in London. He leapt and flew and bounced, and he had now developed a new method of propulsion which we called 'kangaroo-ing'. To do this he sat up very straight, folded his hands against his chest, as if he were begging and in this position leapt fast and furious to his destination. I have never seen any other kind of bush-baby jump in exactly the same way.

But, alas, in London his unfortunate urinating habit was more noticeable than ever. In the country we have natural oak doors and windows, but in London they are rather stupidly painted cream; and when Fricky had been up on some of the smutty cupboard tops with moist hands, and had then bounced on to the painted doors, it was something like the passing of the Fairy Coalman. So not only did I have to go round with my furniture polish, but also with a sponge and leather, and a ladder for the higher places. I had come to love him so much by this time that I didn't grudge it in the least.

In London both Fricky and Infestus were firmly shut in the bathroom at night, but in the country I used to let Fricky bounce round my bedroom, because there was more leap-way for him. The first time I was assured that he really had got to know and love me was when I woke up in the morning and found him curled up asleep on my neck. A greater compliment than this no bush-baby can pay you.

However, I soon found that my curtains were taking such a caning from this all-night session that when I went to bed he was confined to the bathroom along with Festie. It is a large bathroom, and he could still swirl madly around. He had always, of course, retired to sleep when I came through to dress in the morning, but one day he came stalking out of his bed again and, dropping on to my shoulder, started to lick my face all over with his long rough tongue. This became a morning ritual, sometimes quite short, but sometimes exceedingly thorough, when he would hold my ear in his sticky hand and peer anxiously into all the corners. By this time he not only tolerated handling, he loved it. When I held him on my lap with a hand round his middle, he would throw himself backwards like a baby playing, and he loved having his neck rubbed, and to have the fur ruffled up the wrong way on his back.

One day when the nicer weather came and the windows of the house were more often open, he found his way out into the garden. I was in utter despair because it was all so natural for a bush-baby to fly about among the trees. He was perfectly camouflaged and how would I ever catch him again? He was out, I should think, for about half an hour this time, but presently he dropped out of one of the trees on to my shoulder, and never in my life have I been so thankful for anything. I spent the whole of the rest of the evening swearing to myself that never, never would I leave a door open again. But with me, alas, it is

Susie washing nylons. This picture demonstrates the imitative powers of the chimpanzee.

Susie at one-and-a-half years old. 'I love you, too.'

always just until the next time. Many times he went out in the garden after this, but he always came back, and presently I almost ceased worrying about him. Almost. But much as I loved him to have this gorgeous liberty, I still feared that there might one day be a call of the wild and I should lose my beloved creature, and he his life. But I need not have worried: I should have known better. I should have known that it is just when one is *not* worrying that disaster sneaks up. That is a lesson that has at last been very, very well taught me.

One day I agreed to take him, with Infestus, up to the Anglia Television studios in Norwich. I had only once been televised, and that had been with a pair of tawny owls. Then I had been interviewed by Aubrey Buxton in a cosy little studio that was rather like a study. Imagine my horror when I found we were to go on 'live' (we had made a film before), in an enormous studio full of frightening machinery, and a roof exactly like the Big Top. Fricky had had no kind of harness on since the day I had cut off the leather torturer, but I had brought a bit of twisted wool and some tape.

He was furious when I tried to concoct a harness for him, when we were safely shut in our dressing room, furious enough to bite me, which I didn't consider a very auspicious start. I poked my head out of the door and shouted to an amiable young lady who had just gone by that I craved above all things a piece of sticking plaster, and she waved a wand. Fricky in the meantime had extricated himself from his Heath-Robinson harness and was bounding gleefully about the dressing room, from time to time gazing at himself in rapt admiration in one or other of the many mirrors. He hopped happily and unsuspectingly on to my shoulder—his tempers were very violent, but swiftly over. Unfortunately, I had a longer memory and, seizing him firmly around the middle I administered a sharp smack on the top of his head with my plastered hand. As on the very few previous occasions that I had smacked him, he stiffened up, closed his eyes, and raised his big black hands in mute appeal.

'Fricky-Pic,' I said sternly, 'I must put some kind of a harness on you. No bite-ies, just love—do you understand?' He opened his flat yellow eyes and looked at me. 'No bite-ies—just love,' had been my way of finally persuading him to stop scarifying my hands. But he considered it very humiliating that I had smacked him, and he was very quiet while I concocted his doubtful harness, and he let me put it on almost without protest. With the silly bit of wool still trailing I popped him back into the beauty case with Festie, so that he could rest his nerves. I wished there was somewhere that I could rest my nerves too. Instead, I went along to the make-up room, where I was somewhat irritated that they made my eyebrows the wrong shape, but couldn't really work up much of a fuss about it. Then I picked up my box and went into the studio.

Apparently we were to be on a programme called 'About Anglia,' and all sorts of things seemed to be going on at the same time. It reminded me of a revolving stage where one sees bits of this, and bits of that, only it was even more confusing. I loathe machinery, and we were in a nightmare of it. I glanced nervously up at the vast roof and thought that if Fricky's ludicrously inadequate harness broke and he flew up there, 'Anglia Television' and I had both had it.

I was taken, my case and I, to sit on a sofa to one side until it was time for us to 'rehearse'—dread thought! A very charming young man introduced himself as my Interviewer, and came to sit with me awhile. It was not long, however, before I realised that he felt that interviewing animals was very much beneath him, and I had a sudden, almost uncontrollable desire to giggle. Instead, I did my best to re-build his *amour-propre*, telling him that it was really quite a distinguished thing to do and that my last Interviewer had been the great Aubrey Buxton. I think it made him feel a little better—I hope so anyway, because, when it came to struggling with my animals before the cameras, he was a tower of strength. Fricky would do nothing he was supposed to, of course, and I couldn't get that terrible roof out of my mind. Infestus, as usual, was splendid, and everybody laughed about his name, and I am told that the programme was good. But the boring thing about live television is that you can't see yourself. Films for that reason are much more fun—

not from my own point of view, because I always look an uncompromising ninety, but the animal shots can be very fascinating.

Shortly after this we were to leave for a holiday in Corsica, and Fricky and Festie were coming, too. There is no quarantine anywhere in the world for monkeys or rats, but one should, to be painfully correct, have a certificate of health. I hadn't bothered with this before, and had travelled halfway round the world with rats, but this time I thought it would be better to be officially correct. So Fricky and Festie, when we started off in the car for Southend, each had an official passport tucked into the flap of mine. We flew the car over to France, and reached Amiens for the night. The town was very full, and we had to try quite a few hotels before we could get a room with a private bath. I think several receptionists thought us pretty potty to walk out at that time of night just because of a bathroom, when we were only breaking our journey for a few hours, but then they had never slept in a room with a rampaging bush-baby!

Finally we made it, in a very modern hotel in the city centre. But the laugh was on us, because the bathroom was so superbly 'modern' that the door into it appeared to be a sort of paper concertina, and we were not in bed ten minutes before Fricky had found his way through that. Unlike a great many bush-babies Fricky liked people—he liked to be around. Unfortunately my husband was in the bed nearest to the bathroom door and it was on to his head that Fricky landed with a plop. After this had happened two or three times even my good tempered spouse felt that something should be done about it, so I heaved myself out of bed, caught poor Fricky, and shut him, much to his disgust, in the gaunt, uninteresting lavatory.

I must say that this was no ordinary motor trip across France. In the way that we must complicate everything, we were dragging a 22-foot cabin-cruiser behind our Rover 100 (nothing but a car with the tank-like qualities of a Rover would pull such a monster), so the next morning we started very early on our way. It was a beautiful morning, but very cold, so we put up most of the windows of the car. I found myself feeling very sleepy, and what I call 'coming and going', in that awful way that one does when trying to fight against sleep. Lord! I thought to myself, getting ready for this trip must have made me a lot more tired than I thought. And then I looked round and there was Stephen sound asleep on the back seat, mouth wide open, at barely seven thirty in the morning.

'Wake up, Stephen!' I said furiously. 'Put all the windows down,' and I wound mine down. That seemed to blow away all our cobwebs, and the rest of the day passed uneventfully.

As it was August and we had not booked a room, not being certain, with our ridiculous load, how many miles we could cover in a day, we had the same game over bathrooms in the hotels again. Finally we managed to get one attached to a single room, and that one my husband took for me.

It was always such fun at the end of a day's journey to let the sleepy animals out into their new quarters. They used to yawn and stretch, and finally waking up, would dash around on a tour of inspection, both of the bedroom and the bathroom, finally ending up at a pan of water that I had already filled for them. This was the nicest part of the day for me, and soaking in a delicious scented bath before dinner, I could watch them both at play. They were really very like Victor Hugo's Grasshopper and Ant: Fricky just delighted to leap and soar and swing, whereas Festie took life a great deal more seriously—the open beauty case was his bed, and anything that he found around the room that he considered useful, such as paper or a stocking, or even my toothbrush, if it happened to fall on the floor, he carefully hoarded away for future use.

As soon as the luggage had been brought in and the coast was clear I opened their box. Just as I said, it's when one is not worrying that disaster sneaks up and I don't think that in all my life I have ever had such a terrible shock—there they were, as always, wrapped in each other's arms—yes, they were there all right, but they were both dead. It is not possible to describe the utter heartbreak I suffered, looking at those two little creatures that had been so full of life and gaiety, that had been my companions for so long, lying there just as though they were

Bear soon after her arrival.

Susie loved the dogs and they tolerated almost anything. Bear was not interested in this particular game.

Yes! Yes! I've checked the petrol, oil and water.

asleep, as indeed they were, but this time it was for ever. I don't know how I found my husband's room to tell him of the tragedy, and I expect I was entirely incoherent. Both he and Stephen were stunned. And then gradually it dawned on all three of us that they must have been dead a long while, that our heavy sleepiness of the morning had come from carbon-monoxide fumes caused by the boat blocking the exhaust pipe of the car when we started, and that the animals on the floor by my feet had got the full brunt of it. They had suffered nothing of course: it was I who was left to suffer. Every animal one has and loves is bound to bring one heartache in the end, and each time one of them dies it leaves a mark. But it also leaves a memory of the love and the gaiety and the simple sweetness that is the soul of a happy animal. Sometimes I wonder if it really cancels out the pain: but when I wonder that, I know that I am in a very stupid mood.

7

Brazilian Interlude:
Pet for a Day

Apart from the various holiday trips which we took, my husband is always making business trips and in 1957 we visited practically every country in South America.

By the time we reached São Paulo, Brazil, I had worn out the word 'fabulous'. I had been bowled over by Caracas, bewitched by Quito, and bewildered by Buenos Aires. There wasn't a pale concrete building scraping the sky that could wring another exclamation from me.

São Paulo is the practical, businesslike mate of romantic, delicious Rio de Janeiro. It bustles along in the temperate mountains, the centre of the great Brazilian coffee trade, while Rio sunbathes dreamily and steamily by its famously beautiful Copacobana Bay. The boast of São Paulo, then, was to be the fastest growing city in the world. It may well have been but I found it exceedingly ugly and monotonous. We were only there for two days, and on those days it rained.

One day we lunched with the British Consul General (he asked me what I thought of São Paulo and I weakly muttered 'fabulous' of course). I enquired what one did in São Paulo in the rain. I can't say that his face exactly lit up with inspiration, but having murmured through the museums, which didn't inspire me either, he suddenly exclaimed 'Butantan'. It sounded like a Brazilian bad word, but I looked enquiring.

'Snake Farm,' he elucidated, brightening visibly.

'Snake Farm?' I repeated stupidly. 'Whatever for?'

'Oh, they milk the poison from them,' he said cheerfully, 'and mix it with horse's blood. Makes an anti-snake-bite serum that they ship all over the Western Hemisphere.'

'It sounds disgusting,' my husband said unhelpfully.

'Well, they say it's reduced snake-bite deaths in Brazil by eighty per cent,' the Consul answered mildly, and we left it at that.

Next day it continued to rain. My husband hustled off to a business appointment, and left me staring out of the window at the deluge. It bucketed down. But after a few minutes watching the white buildings smudge back into the mist I took a pull on myself. However one spent a day in São Paulo, rain or no rain, mooning in a hotel bedroom was bottom of the list. Not that it wasn't a magnificent bedroom, in the brilliant Jaragua (pronounced like an angry snarl) Hotel, because it had been reserved for an Ambassadress: I had even had her huge exotic bouquet of flowers, until, to my disgust, my husband had forced me to unbelt—it was a delicious affair of green carnations, pale orchids, improbable bullrushes and crimson love-lies-bleeding.

Like the Jaragua, I snarled at the rain. Then I suddenly thought of Butantan. I didn't think snakes and rain were much of a combination, but the name appealed to me and I thought that the snakes, whilst not appealing, might be interesting.

'Butantan,' I chanted, buckling on my old Rolleiflex, which gives me the same sort of courage that 'packing a rod' must give to a nervous gunman.

At the reception desk I hired myself a taxi for the morning —I didn't fancy being stranded in a Snake Farm. We drove out through one of the older residential districts, wide avenues of lovely Spanish style villas, set in charming gardens, shaded by jacaranda, oleander and palm; and because of the height, the grass was green and the roses were in bud. After a while we plunged out into scrubby, scruffy country, and then, quite suddenly, swept into Butantan. Equally suddenly I realised that I hadn't given a thought to how I was going to get to see anything, and I'm way past thinking the innocent tourist normally gets to see anything at all. So, as we drove up the fine, palm-lined drive, I scratched hopefully in my bag. As luck would have it I found a card the Press Officer in Caracas had given me (let's hope with his love), and under his name were printed the impressive words 'Secretary to Her Britannic Majesty's Embassy'. Just for the hell of it I wrote my name at the top, and 'Butantan' at the bottom and hoped that some simple soul would be impressed.

We pulled up in front of a building, faintly reminiscent of the White House, Washington. When the driver turned to me I handed him my card, saying, I hoped with authority, 'El Senhor Director, fash favor'. He took the card and studied it gravely, though I don't suppose he could read, then, giving me a brilliant smile, he slid out of the car and plunged into the building. I waited curiously. In minutes he was out again, followed by an ancient porter, toothless and negroid, who was now holding my deceitful card; but there was no question of his reading it, unless he was some quaint genius who did it upside down for the sheer pleasure of the thing!

'El Senhor Director etc.' I repeated, firmer yet, and was rewarded by a gappy grin and a thumb sign to come inside. We went up in a lift and traipsed along endless corridors, until we found a woman secretary whose English precisely tallied with my Portuguese; but even this was an encouraging oasis.

'El Senhor Director on meeting,' she said, sadly shaking her head. I only wanted, I murmured, equally sadly, to see the Snake Pits. At this she brightened, twittered to the porter, seized my hand, and patting it kindly, repeated 'other doctor, other doctor' half a dozen times. Not to be outdone, I thanked her half a dozen times and then we went in search of 'other doctor.' But when we found him 'other doctor' wasn't playing ball—maybe not being 'on meeting' had turned him sour. So we traipsed back to the hall.

Here, with encouraging smiles, I was asked to wait 'un momento' which I didn't like one bit. I have waited some 'momentos' in my time and frankly it's a most unrewarding pastime. Just as I was wondering how long I would allow this moment to become, up the steps sprang a white-coated figure, young, dark and be-spectacled.

Bear, still small enough to be in the house.

I don't think you've had the pleasure of meeting one of my friend's ancestors.

'Doctor Belluomini, English very bad,' he said breathlessly, and burst out laughing.

'Wonderful that you speak at all,' I replied, and meant it. The bouncy little doctor looked charmed. He also looked full enough of fun and enthusiasm to defy the dreary day. And I was really in luck, because he was Head of the Snake Department, I discovered, for Butantan, which being an enterprising Institute, goes in also for such horrors as scorpions, tarantulas, and enormous poison frogs. Belluomini cocked an eye at my Rolleiflex. 'Colour?' he asked. 'No,' I replied, still being a sucker for black and white. 'Good,' he said, glancing at the tedious day, 'we try.'

We left the Presidential Residence and crossed a garden to a small green shed. Out of this emerged a dark man, with a sad, questioning look.

'He's been bitten five times,' said Belluomini, with pride. Heavens, I thought, no wonder he has a sad, questioning look.

After a short conference this sad man fetched a wooden box from the hut, dragged a huge rattlesnake out of it and flung it on the ground. I felt a twinge of pity for the rattler as it twisted rather hopelessly on the ground, but I suppose if I had been bitten five times, my thoughts would have been quite otherwise. At a sign from the doctor, the dark man fished the creature up and, very bravely it seemed to me, with thumb and forefinger on either side of its head, forced its jaws open with a pair of tweezers, and hung its fangs over a glass. After a short pause, out came the poison—drip, drip, drip into the waiting glass. All ready to be mixed with horse blood to make the life-saving serum. I hastened to photograph the sad man who gazed back mournfully at me, now grasping the great snake by head and tail, which clamped its jaws shut and rattled away like mad.

After this angry creature had been pushed back into its box, a lovely soft blue Mussurana was slithered on to the ground. Alas, all lovely thoughts were swept away by the perfectly fearful smell of it, something to do with sex, if I understood my doctor correctly; indeed, I was to learn that sex played quite a part in a snake's short life.

Next Jão (the sad!) came out holding in his hands a long, deliciously marked snake, delicately criss-crossed and banded with red, white and black. This was a False Coral, False here being a happy term, meaning non-venomous, because the True Coral, which is slightly smaller and not quite so brilliant, is the most utterly lethal of all South America's snakes.

'Lovely!' I cried, rapidly becoming a 'snakeophile', and indeed, I did find it beautiful.

'Yes, pretty,' nodded the doctor, and abruptly seizing the creature from Jão he thrust it into my arms. Startled, and quite horrified, I somehow grasped it amidships, at the same time trying to look as though snakes and I were just like that together. After the first moment of shock, I was astonished and charmed by the feel of it, so cool, and smooth and dry. It wriggled itself around, and looked thoughtfully into my face. 'But you're really rather sweet,' I thought, 'with your boot-button eyes, and patent-leather nose!' I suppose I must have been smiling at it foolishly as well, because the doctor asked eagerly, 'You like?'

'Oh yes, very much,' I said, trying to stop it winding itself round my neck.

'Then you have!' he cried triumphantly, and before I could protest or indeed say anything at all, it had been stuffed in what to me seemed a very inadequate box and done up as a parcel.

'But what does it eat?' I asked anxiously, suddenly realising that I was now the rather stunned owner of a snake.

'Oh, live mice,' was the grisly and unequivocal reply.

'But where on earth would I get them?' I wailed, letting my I.Q. down to the bottom of a snake pit.

'Laboratories,' was the laconic reply. 'One month, two month, he not eat. Only water. Then live mice.'

I swallowed, quite overcome by my appalling liability, nevertheless tucking the neat box meekly under my arm.

'And here,' cried the doctor delightfully, 'is for luck,' and he rattled a rattler's rattle at me gleefully, before dropping it into my, by then, nervous hand. It was like seven pieces of dried sweet corn, threaded loosely together, the dryness and the looseness, plus a furious current from its body, adding up to the rattler's truly sinister warning.

'Now for the pits,' said the irrepressible Belluomini, gently relieving me of my cardboard box. And so to the pits we went. They were not in the least as I had expected them—'snake pit' conjures up horrible visions. But no snake had any grumble here. The pits were indeed sunk, but they were beautifully grassed, and dotted with flowering trees for the snakes to climb, and circular terra-cotta shelters to protect them from the sun. There were three of these gardens, which is a far more accurate description—one for venomous, and two for non-venomous snakes. Crouched amongst the curled and slumberous forms of the venomous were some of the vastest and most hideous frogs I have ever seen, with nightmare mouths and bulging eyes. These were the poison frogs; the venomous snakes, by some strange sort of arrangement, leave them strictly alone, whereas, to quote Belluomini, harmless snakes 'eat poison frogs like cocktail'.

Poor João had by now marched manfully into the arena, and was prodding the rattlers awake, who struck lazily at his leather covered ankles. But from Belluomini I learnt, in his inimitable English, that the harmless snakes are far more 'aggressible' than the poisonous ones, far quicker to anger and attack.

Now we walked down a palm-lined drive to the museum. There were coffee bushes growing amongst the palms—'For tourist,' said Belluomini lightly, which made me feel non-tourist and pretty smug. As Head of the Snake Department he naturally showed me the Snake Section first. It was a very comprehensive one, with an alarming illustrated history of snake bites. To my surprise I found that the rattler was a comparatively nice chap —he just kills you. But the Mussurana group, on the other hand, starts off by destroying the flesh tissue, an incredibly painful process. There were two quite ghastly human legs in pickle to prove it, one with the flesh white and bloated, rolling down to the ankle; and one with the flesh turned black, just by way of a change. There were photographs of people who had lost arms and feet and fingers in this unattractive way, so, added to their repulsive smell, I decided I didn't care much for the Mussurana group.

We then moved on to scorpions, other creatures of unpleasing habits; the black scorpion (that looked a dirty brown to me) attacks men working in the fields, whilst its yellow opposite number attends to the women and children at home. Next came fantastic great hairy spiders—the sort one could borrow (at some risk) for a pantomime. I was just musing on this when the words 'Scotland Yard' brought me back with a bump. Belluomini was pointing, not to the live spiders, but to giant model ones sitting on giant model webs. I guarantee nothing, but I think this is what he said:

'Scotland Yard has some of these nasty creatures, and when there is a narcotics murder, flies are soaked in the blood of the corpse and fed to the spiders. According to the lethal narcotic used, morphia, heroin, etc., the spiders, under the influence of it, spin the appropriate web.' According to the doctor it is infallible.

At that moment, woken from thralldom, I discovered it was one o'clock.

'Heavens!' I exclaimed. 'I really have kept you much too long and I'm pretty late myself.'

'But you must see my laboratory,' he said reproachfully. 'It takes no time.' This I did not believe and I dislike laboratories, but he had been so very kind that I could scarcely refuse. I think what he really wanted to show me was an extremely inelegant muddle of bi-sexual snakes (sex with us again) on which he had written an impressive paper. He presented me proudly with an English translation, but for all it conveyed to me it might just as well have stayed in its original Portuguese.

Then he showed me an unbelievable frog, and to this very day I wish he hadn't: its cry, like that of an anguished child, haunts me yet. It was an enormous mottled great thing the size of a pekingese, with a great green stripe down its back, and the biggest, pinkest lined mouth I have ever seen; and out of this sickening cavity came that dreadful tortured appeal.

'Oh, don't prod it any more please!' I begged, as he approached it again. And this time I really insisted on going.

He saw me to my car, and I thanked him sincerely for a fascinating morning, and promised to look him up on my next visit to Brazil, a promise I very much hope to implement. I waved until he was only a small white figure at the end of a long avenue, then leaned over and picked up the ridiculously small square box. If only it had not been for that fearful diet of mice!

My husband was waiting for me, crotchety and sour-faced, when I burst into the Ambassadorial room, gaily waving my box.

'I've had a wonderful morning and I've got a snake!' I cried.

'Don't be so silly,' said my husband. 'You have kept me waiting for lunch.'

'But I *have* got a snake,' I retorted, starting to undo the box. He looked at me with more attention then, and came to peer over my shoulder. There, curled round in perfect coils was the beautiful Coral, and as I started to pick it up, my husband leapt back, horrified. The snake twisted itself round my arm and shot out its tongue in anxious exploration.

'It will bite!' yelled my husband, taking a few more leaps to the rear.

'Oh no it won't,' I answered with complete assurance. I knew my little doctor wouldn't dream of getting me bitten.

'Put it back. You are not going to keep it. You must be mad. I want my lunch.' My husband speaks in telegram idiom when really upset, and 'really' was the word for it now. I laughed, but I curled my lovely Coral neatly back into the box in which he seemed quite happy, and, finally, we had our lunch.

During this delayed meal I graciously agreed to send back my snake, with the one small proviso, that my husband should buy me one of the enchanting pieces of Brazilian jewellery over which I had been drooling for the past twenty-four hours. I have to admit that it was a most dishonest bargain, because, much as I would have loved to keep the decorative creature, I could never have faced a future of feeding one live animal to another, especially when thinking of my beloved white rats.

'I'll just photograph him while you are out, and by the time you get back—with my brooch of course—he'll be gone,' I said soothingly.

So I spent a happy afternoon photographing my snake, who was a charming model, gentle, patient and co-operative. For a prop, I decided on my white umbrella, which he found pleasant to twist himself around, and when I had let off three films and done prodding the poor thing, he wound himself comfortably around it, and went to sleep. Perhaps, indeed, he thought it the branch of a tree. All the time I was packing (we were leaving that night) he slept there, peacefully and majestically beautiful, and, but for those wretched mice, nothing would have driven me to send him back. He was still asleep when my husband returned, unexpectedly early.

'Oh no!' he cried, catching sight of him at once, so I quieted him with the kind little doctor's telephone number. I don't suppose Belluomini was really very surprised by the ungracious return of his gift, because he just laughed and said airily 'Leave it with porter. I fetch.'

So I curled my snake, that wasn't mine any more, back into his box as comfortably as I could, after giving him a long cool drink of water. And as we passed through the hall on our way to the airport, we handed this innocent looking parcel to the porter, marked 'This side up', and, for their own sakes, 'With care.'

This was the only part of the whole affair that my husband enjoyed—he found it extremely funny. I didn't find it funny at all, but I must say I drew a good deal of comfort from the exquisite circle of all the Brazilian stones that was now pinned to me. For they also were very beautiful; and above all they required no mice.

8

A Chimpanzee Around the House

Never had I wished to possess a parrot or a monkey. That is a sweeping statement, I know—so many different parrots, hundreds of different monkeys, but that's the way it was. But the surprising advent of Susie was to teach me just how fascinating a baby chimpanzee, at any rate, can be.

It is a strange feeling when, for the first time, a chimpanzee leaps into your arms, wraps its own immensely long ones round you, and lays its funny wrinkled little face trustingly under your chin. Among other sensations is one of warm compact strength. They smell sweet—no monkey smell here—only the pleasant tang of warm young animal. But I must confess that when, greatly thrilled, I first held Susie in my arms, I had absolutely no idea of all that lay before us.

Susie was a white-faced chimpanzee, which means that her face was the colour of a well-baked biscuit. She was very beautiful chimpwise, and I was delighted with her. Twelve hours later I was a good deal less delighted, as nothing and nobody could prise her off me.

The strength of that small square block of bone and muscle was fantastic, and the long fingers gripped me like steel. In her bewildered world I had become the mother figure. And don't imagine that she wasn't heavy, even then. That was something I could vouch for, as I staggered on hour after hour with Susie firmly clamped to some part of my anatomy. Finally, exhausted, I trudged upstairs, and undressing somehow, flopped us both into bed. Once on the bed, for the first time in hours, the terrible grip relaxed, and with sudden hope I tried to roll off the bed. More fool me! As if, I thought bitterly, I could beat the agility of an ape. But presently she settled down, with her hands laid gently, in readiness, against my back, her little head on the pillow, and softly snoring, off she went to sleep. She was quite clean all night and as long as I didn't stir, neither did she. All things considered we slept very well.

This may sound an odd way to start chimpanzee-keeping, but most of my animals arrive suddenly and inadvertently, and, as far as is possible, are allowed to choose where, and with whom, they want to live. Susie quite definitely picked on me and my bedroom, and for the first few weeks, though very funny, this was rather trying. Not for a moment would she let me out of her sight, not even through the open bathroom door. If she thought I was making for the main door, she would manacle my ankles with her steel hawser arms, or raise pathetic pale hands appealingly so that I should pick her up. There is something completely heart-rending about a baby chimpanzee, until it loses its temper. Suddenly it sits down, opens its quite hideous great mouth, full of large white teeth, and emits ear-splitting screams, while furiously pounding its clenched fists on the ground. Susie's abrupt change from an adorable and appealing waif, to a noisy and horrible gargoyle, used to make me laugh. And the more I laughed, the louder (if possible) she screamed. And the more she screamed, the more I laughed. It is said that the true basis of humour is the monstrous and the absurd: that being so there can be nothing funnier than a chimpanzee in a temper.

At first I thought she would be too much, even for me, because next day the clinging vine act continued unabated. But gradually, little by little, the nervous terror of the grip relaxed, and, as long as she had one arm round my ankle, she was prepared to hobble after me, which meant that we both hobbled; it was a vast improvement on carrying the whole dead weight of her.

We worked out a bedroom routine too. She would wake up at about half-past seven in the morning, and be firmly sat on a baby's potty. This she thought was quite fun, but if not carefully watched, she would gaily turn it upside down afterwards.

Wait for me, I'm just picking up speed.

Oops!

Bear's snout for ant catching can be seen clearly in this excellent photograph.

Then she sat on a little table by my bed and ate a fruit breakfast, and drank milk out of a bottle, which, when empty, she laid tenderly on its side: she was always very careful with cups and bottles. While eating her breakfast she made contented little noises, 'Umm-umm, umm-umm', and 'Hu-hu, hu-hu'. She had beautiful table manners, quite unlike my beloved Fricky-Pic, who had none at all. And whereas Fricky's black hands were coarse and knuckly, Susie's were elegance itself, long and tapered, with beautifully formed small nails. In fact they reminded me of the hands of some women with dreadful long, long nails, because although her nails were not long the general impression was the same. But this is probably just sour grapes, because my hands are square and pudgy.

When the 'Umm-umm' breakfast was finished, she would climb slowly off the table on to my bed, where I was probably finishing mine, and creep in beside me. Every mouthful I took she followed with her intense dark eyes, and then she would gaze up into my face, almost reverently, as though I had accomplished something miraculous by swallowing a few pieces of very dull biscuit. With our respective breakfasts over, the next move was to the bathroom.

This was the highlight of Susie's day. Fortunately I have a large bathroom, with a large basin. She used to pull herself up, and sit, Mandarin fashion, on the edge of this, utterly enthralled with the whole business of tooth cleaning, face washing, nail scrubbing. She watched me with the same avid concentration as when I was performing that magical trick of eating my breakfast. But after a few days—which under the circumstances was quite a long time—watching alone was not good enough: Susie was tired of spectator sports. So, one morning, instead of following me to the bath, she remained seated on the basin, and, picking up the sponge, she started to wash her face. After the first bash, with the unaccustomed water dripping down her face, she looked earnestly at the sponge in her hand, as though it had played her a dirty trick, or at any rate had done the unexpected. But, full of courage, she tried again. This time was far worse, because she was rather violent in her determination not to be beaten, and the water went up her funny flat nose. Sneezing violently, she flung the sponge down in disgust and galloped over to the bath. I hitched a towel off the rail, and carefully dried the anxious, puzzled little face. She enjoyed that, standing there with her hands gripping the edge of the bath. When I had done, she continued to gaze at me.

There is something very disconcerting about being studied by a chimpanzee, whether in the bath or out. It is not so much the somewhat human shape of the face, as the curious, inscrutable expression in the large wide eyes. 'How much is she taking in and what is she making of it?' one wonders gloomily. Is it just a blank semi-idiot stare, or is it a deeply intelligent one, and if so, what thoughts are going on in that funny, coconut shaped head? Is it admiration or contempt that she is feeling? And that is a thing I never clearly decided in all the long while I had Susie.

Face washing did not become a success, even with practice. But tooth cleaning was something else again: there was no sudden shock of water going in the wrong direction, some toothpastes tasted delicious, and there was always the brush to have a good chew on, when scrubbing it backwards and forwards had lost its charm. And washing nylon undies was most exciting. There were four hands—hers and mine—in the basin, all sorts of things swirling back and forth, and a cover of fascinating bubbles on the top. It must be admitted that during Susie's time I did not make my appearance in the sane world very early in the morning.

Apart from raiding the larder, playing in the bathroom was Susie's first love, her idea of a heaven on earth and her favourite pastime. Almost anything else that took her passing fancy in the way of playing she soon tired of, but she would spend a whole morning with me in that confined space if I could ever find enough to do to spend a whole morning there.

When we had finished our water games, I would dry her very carefully, because when she came she was rather bald. She had nasty bare patches on her head, too, where I rubbed in a hair restorer, until I found the smell so repulsive that I settled for the bare patches. I needn't have worried anyway. I have a theory that as long as monkeys are protected from damp and draught, they can stand a great deal of cold and it makes their coats grow. In Susie's case it certainly did, because she later slept in a very cold room, and grew a wonderfully long thick silky coat, and all the scruffy patches on her head were covered up.

When she was small, Susie was astonishingly obedient. I only had to say: 'Down, Susie,' for her to drop to the floor; or even more quickly answered was my warning, 'I'm going, Susie', for her to drop everything, even food, to rush to me with out-stretched arms. In this way I dissuaded her from climbing up the curtains, and from carefully taking down the porcelain plates and bowls that stood about; indeed, people who came to our house were astonished to see open cabinets of porcelain, and Battersea enamels standing on the mantlepiece, while a baby chimpanzee went clambering around, but there never were any accidents to them in Susie's time any more than when Fricky was bouncing round.

During this time we were having a floor to ceiling cage built for her in a warm corner of the animal room. I thoroughly dis-like cages, but this is probably not entirely justified in the case of wild animals, who cannot, owing to climate and many other reasons, be at liberty. They must be given a sense of security, and the first step to feeling secure is a home of one's own. This is a lesson I learnt early on, and I have never since been un-duly worried about cages, provided they are spacious and clean. This cage was a nice large one, and we made a wooden seat and a bar for her to swing on. We put her travelling cage in as a bed, because she could stretch out to full length in it, and it was warm and dark. Just like children, baby chimps sleep right through a long night, and the first morning I went down to fetch her at half past seven, there was no sign of her at all. She proved that she was there by the gentle snoring which emanated from her bedroom.

For the first few weeks in her new home, I fetched her every morning at eight o'clock and took her upstairs for her breakfast and the bathroom drill. But gradually she got used to eating in her cage, and to having more strenuous exercise round the house, because of course, she was growing rapidly.

One of her favourite games was to race along the landing from my bedroom, and, without pause, to fling herself from the top to the bottom of the bare oak stairs. The first time I saw her do this, I was exceedingly alarmed. The trouble with a chimp is that one comes to identify it with a child, and I shudder to think what state a child would have been in, who had done what Susie did many times daily, just for the hell of it. On this first occasion, I rushed to the head of the stairs, fully expecting to see a limping and suitably chastened little chimp creeping up the stairs for comfort. Quite the contrary, when she caught sight of me, with added *bravura*, she turned a somersault on the half-landing and crashed down the rest of the hard unforgiving oak treads. To say that I was flabbergasted is an understatement. I could not understand how anything of flesh and blood could take such a battering, and for the pleasure of it— and yet even more incredible would it be that an animal would purposely do itself daily hurt. Then I remembered how, when she had first leapt into my arms, her solid chunky body had impressed me. She felt like no other animal I had ever handled: like steel. I was to remember this once again when the time came that I had to chastise her: there is no other word for it, because there is not much future in smacking a lump of concrete.

Another favourite amusement of Sue's was, when hearing any of the dogs coming up the stairs, to beat them to it by racing along the landing, and there at the top to do a furious jungle war dance, pounding her hands and feet violently on the parquet, and huffing in their faces. This was most effective. Usually the dogs would turn around and go slowly back down the stairs, in which case this imp of mischief would roll down on top of them, scattering them in all directions. This was real 'custard-pie' comedy, and it enchanted me. But she more than met her match when my old pekingese, Pekaboo, came bobbing up the stairs.

Pekaboo's method of getting up the stairs is all his own. They

Bear at the wheel of the Land-Rover.
Slightly exhausted after galloping.

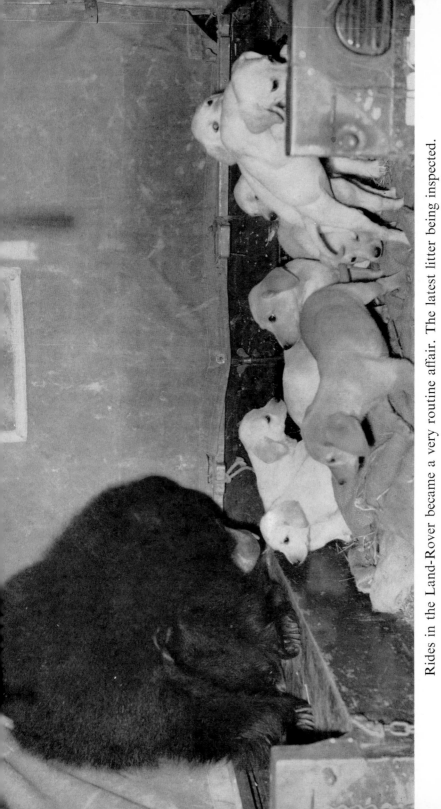

Rides in the Land-Rover became a very routine affair. The latest litter being inspected.

are extremely slippery, and his legs are very short, therefore a goodly impetus is needed to carry him to the top. If he gets impeded, he gets stuck, and a good deal of effort is required for him to get under way again. When, in full flight upwards, he became aware of Susie and her King-Kong act, he took not the slightest notice. This caught Susie unawares the first time it happened, so spectacular had her success with the bigger dogs been, so Pekaboo cannoned into her block-like body and fell backwards down the stairs. Fury blazed in his large dark eyes, and with a terrific effort, he started upwards once more. Susie was not so sure this time, so she withdrew a little. Pekaboo made the top, and promptly bit her with his few remaining teeth. Susie got the message and, from then on, Pekaboo was able to continue his careful method of getting up the stairs.

By this time Susie had become used to her routine in the cage. She was always fed in it, and after a spell of liberty she was always certain of finding some delicious bits and pieces—cake, a bottle of fizzy orange, or milk and fruit. Whenever I was at home I gave her all the freedom that was possible around the house, and she really behaved wonderfully. It was a long, damp, dreary winter, and there was no question of taking her outside for her exercise; but I used to dream of the spring, when she would be able to go out, and swing in the trees, and play on the lawn with the dogs. Once she had had a spring and summer out, I felt she would be quite hardy enough to take the winter too, all but the dampest days, so that when she was in a tiresome mood, and irritated me around the house, as indeed it was inevitable that she should, I just thought of the lovely life ahead for her, and was as patient as I could be.

But as I have said, she really was wonderful, considering her natural curiosity, her pent-up energy, and the fascinating things into which she could get her hands and feet. After we had taken as much exercise as possible, if I wanted to write letters, I would sit her on the floor beside me with a collection of things to play with, usually including a bottle of fizzy orange juice with the top on. Tops take hours to get off! Then when she was bored with all her playthings, I used to call to her, 'I'm going, Susie', and she would hasten after me and we would go along to the animal room. Nearly always she would go into her cage because she liked to do so, but chimps are remarkably moody. Just occasionally, when she was in a bad mood, or even more occasionally, when she had raided the larder, and was not in the least bit tempted by the food that had been laid out for her in the cage, go in she would not. The battle that then followed would be long, exhausting, and frankly infuriating. She had all the strength, but I had the greater determination. One day, after we had wrestled for what seemed hours (I never once gave in, as I knew how fatal that would be) experimentally, she bit me in the arm. It was just a light bite, and only bruised me— I would in no wise have fancied a full-scale bite from that impressive jawful of huge white teeth—but for that tentative bite, I gave her a good sound walloping. I hated doing it and her screams were terrible, though thinking back to those stairs, I am sure they were uttered in fright, and not in pain. The fright was that I had never laid a finger on her before, but then neither had she, ever before, attempted to attack me. In both cases it was the first time and the last time, and ever afterwards she always went into her cage for me without any fuss at all. With other people she could still be tiresome, but gradually, even with them, she became very much more tractable.

As with so many of my stranger animals, the labradors were a great help with Susie. Old Binna was still there, with now another daughter, and a son of Itsy's called Bruce. All three rather liked Susie, though sometimes she did pull their ears a little harder than was comfortable. But they didn't mind her rolling over them, or doing balancing acts on their backs, and they were quite patient when she carefully opened their eyes when they were asleep, or pushed an exploratory finger in between their teeth. And when, in the day, she was put in her cage, one or other of the labradors would be shut in with her so that she would not be lonely.

Finally, and very late, the day that I had so much looked forward to arrived. Spring! A beautiful soft day with no wind, and the grass warm and dry. I stretched out my arms to Susie, and as usual in she jumped, and round my neck went her long warm arms. Triumphantly I flung open the garden door, and we advanced into the great out-of-doors. We also, incidentally, advanced into what was going to prove a great disappointment to me.

Susie's first reaction was to tighten her arms around my neck, and hide her face against me. There was nothing very odd about this because, of course, everything was strange to her, since she had always been indoors. But nothing would induce her to get down on the grass, and I began to be reminded of those awful first days, and the vice-like grip I had suffered then. So our first outing in the glorious spring sunshine turned out to be nothing more exhilarating than a plod around the garden with Susie clamped against me like a solid block of iron.

'Well, you are a silly old girl!' I said to her when we got in. 'Lovely trees, lovely green grass. You're like a slum child.' She studied my face gravely, as she always did when I spoke to her, and the dark, opaque unblinking eyes appeared to take in and absorb everything I said and meant. But how much did she really absorb, I wondered, as she raised one delicate forefinger, carefully traced the line of my then still mouth, and then put her hands over her face.

For a wonderful change we had a spell of radiant weather, and we were able to go out every day. And presently I was able to persuade Susie to get down from me, and to run about on the grass. But, quite definitely, she did not like it. Even more did she dislike the stones of the drive; and those trees, that in my imagination were going to fill her with such joy, I think she regarded as spiky, unpleasant monstrosities that had nothing to do with her.

By this time she was tall enough to open the garden door and it is sad to relate that her longest run over the precious grass was to reach this door, to wrench it open, and to disappear rapidly into the house. I foiled her here by locking the door, so she used to gallop wildly round the house looking for open windows. At first it was only the downstairs windows, and it was fairly easy to see that those were shut. But presently she found she could climb up the lead pipes and in through the upstairs windows. But what made it rather trying was that by the time I ran her to earth in the house, she had nearly always raided the larder before I could get there, and on several occasions had emptied the refrigerator.

As she grew older and stronger, nothing could keep Susie out of the house. She came to know every loose window, every unlocked door. Even our front door, which is so 'olde worlde' that guests have the greatest difficulty in struggling in, presented her with no problems and she was perfectly capable of opening it. But the highlight of her cat-burgling activities took place on a day when I was determined to take the dogs for a walk, and determined that Susie should come too. Quite often I would leave her indoors with Doris, our cook, in the afternoon, while she was having a rest. Susie quite enjoyed an afternoon siesta, and would fall sound asleep on the bed beside her for an hour or two. But this day Doris was not feeling well, and a chimpanzee is no rest cure any time at all. So I locked up, shut up, bolted up—everywhere—and then said to Susie 'There. Now walkies it is, and serve you right.' Unfortunately, the only person who was going to be served right over this small contretemps was me.

All went well for some twenty minutes, and then I discovered that Susie was no longer trailing along behind us, in her usual brassed-off fashion. Nowhere to be seen, in fact. 'Oh well,' I thought, 'there's not a lock or a bar or a bolt unlocked, unpinned, or unshot. She can just wander around the house until we get back.' So quickening to a more agreeable pace, off we went, seven dogs and myself that is, for a stinging walk. I must admit we were away for quite a while, but when we returned, the pandemonium that greeted us was entirely unexpected.

Susie, it seemed, had belted back to the house, and had systematically tried every existing form of entry, but, as I knew, all to no avail. She had, however, made her mind up to get in, and she intended that nothing should stop her. First of all she shinned up the lead pipes leading on to the roof just by Doris's bedroom window. Susie tried the window, but it was firmly

The daily walk with the dogs was always an event.

Bear sucking her paw and humming with contentment.

Alone at last.

barred against her. So she flattened her nose against the panes to make quite sure that there was someone in the room, and when her angry rattling was ignored, she hopped up above the window, and calmly proceeded to take the tiles off the roof and to throw them on to the terrace below. Fortunately, before she actually entered the house by this unorthodox route, somebody heard the luckless tiles crashing to the ground, and rushed round with a ladder to climb up and prise her off the roof. But Susie had made her point—and there was a little matter of some thirty pounds worth of damage to the roof, to underline it. Susie was in disgrace for some while after this, and saw a good deal more of the inside of her cage than she had done previously.

9

Enter Bear

Soon after this escapade with Susie, I acquired yet another wild animal. Well, acquired is perhaps the wrong word; this next wild animal was really thrust upon me. I had returned to my London flat after having had my hair done, only to find a medium sized wicker basket outside the flat door. From inside came noises, and I investigated!

My first meeting with Bear was as startling as it was bloody. When I pulled back the pin of the wicker basket she came out like a jack-in-the-box, and caught me smartly between the eyes. Jack-in-the-box she looked too, with a huge, ungainly head, enormous claws, and a body that tapered away to absolutely nothing. She only had small teeth then, but they were adequate, and the claw which raked across my forehead, for good measure, did little for my looks. Dripping with blood and furious at this onslaught I restuffed her into the wicker basket, then breathing deeply, sat down to consider what I should do about this obviously terrified and quite hideous arrival. For Bear was really ugly then, scruffy and grotesque. Perhaps she wasn't ever very beautiful, but she had a lovely coat, and grew to fit those fearsome claws. Anyway, I became extremely fond of her, which probably provided the rose coloured spectacles that certainly did not exist for her at first.

She arrived in the late afternoon in London, when I was due down for a dinner and dance in Suffolk, for which I had invited an old friend, as my husband was away. So hastily gathering up my things, and my protesting basket, I took a taxi to Liverpool Street Station.

This was to prove a nicely wasted effort, as Bear spent the intervening traffic-blocked time weakening the wicker basket with her struggles, and working herself up into such a frenzy that her cries sounded as though I had a terrified drunk concealed about me some place. When we finally reached the ticket barrier, there was no disguising the agonised 'Oo-er—Oo-er' that was coming from the heaving basket, and even I had not the nerve to declare it was a puppy. The ticket collector decided that she must travel in the guard's van, and theoretically that of course was fine: but to take an animal in the guard's van it must, by the laws of red-tape, be transformed into a parcel.

The whole of London seemed to have converged on Liverpool Street Station that evening, and by the time we had struggled to the Parcels' Office a large piece of rubbery nose was sticking out, and we had missed at least three trains. I had to face the fact that no guard was going to be very keen on this piece of emerging livestock, so after a moment or two of dithering I gave it up, and, accompanied by the incessant 'Oo-er' I beat it for another taxi, and back to the comparative shelter of the flat. What had happened to poor Charles English who was supposedly waiting for me in Suffolk I had no idea, and I am ashamed to say this was not the greatest of my worries. I eventually persuaded a car hire firm to produce a car, without of course explaining the joy that lay ahead for them.

Being Friday the road was a nightmare of traffic. We stopped and started and bumped and bored, and it was not long before Bear was out of her flimsy basket and rampaging round the back of the car. The chauffeur was in luck because he had a glass partition, but at one moment on our crowded way we were stopped at a police block—put up, no doubt, for the usual escaped prisoner from Chelmsford Gaol—but to my lasting disappointment the sergeant only flashed a torch in on us. His reception, had he been a little more inquisitive, would more than have made up for the hell I was going through, but delicious things like that never seem to happen to me. We were waved on, and reached home without further trouble. Except, of course, for the trouble of fifteen pounds worth of damage done to that reluctant Daimler!

So there I was with a bear. One day, perhaps, I shall know what animals are coming, and from where, and just how dangerous or destructive they may be. I shall be ready to greet them with splendid cages and correct diets and much knowledge acquired from the study of animals in captivity. This will be sensible and correct and well organised, and in every way admirable, but somehow, in the back of my mind there lurks a doubt. Will we ever get to know each other quite so well, or come to be on quite such give-and-take terms as when we have to apologise to one another for mistakes about the house: they, perhaps, because they have been dirty, or have bitten me, and I, because I have given them something that has made them sick, or too hot, or too cold, before we have worked out a routine, and have come by trial and error to a happy way of life, which is by no means always that which would be recommended by the voice of knowledge.

That night, or rather in the early hours of the morning, having apologised very humbly to my kind and forgiving friend Charles, who came down in a dressing-gown to find out what on earth had happened to me, there didn't seem much to be done about Bear except to take her to bed with me. I let the oddly shaped little creature scuttle about my room while I undressed, and then made to go downstairs to find her some bread and milk. Bread and milk seems the universal answer to first feeding problems, though for all I knew she might well thrive on minced nails and battery acid—my face was feeling a little as though she did do by this time. But Bear wasn't letting me leave the room without her, at any price. By that time, in the strange way which seems to happen with wild animals out of their element, I had become the one fixed thing in her bewildered and frightened world, and that thing she was sticking to, come what might.

Clumsily at my heels she made it to the top of the stairs, where there seemed nothing for it but to pick her up. To my surprise, and I must say considerable relief, she neither bit nor scratched me, but wrapped her awkward claws carefully round my bare arm, and only puffed a little anxiously as we descended the stairs. Bread and milk seemed to be the right thing after all, and she sucked it up noisily, messily and gratefully; and since we were both by this time pretty well exhausted all that was left was to collect the animal blankets and for us both to fall into bed. I suppose she slept well, for I know I did, and when I awoke in the morning she was still curled up beside me in a black untidy ball.

Looking back on those early days, the thing I remember most vividly was my puzzlement over the extraordinary shape of her. Often, as I watched her scrabbling along in front of me, I would come to the depressing conclusion that she would never grow at all behind, but would get larger and larger in the head like some repulsive dwarf. Sometimes friends, who were interested in animals, would walk with me, and invariably they asked, 'Should she really look like that?' I could only answer sadly that I didn't know, because experts, to whom I appealed, were not much interested in what she looked like, but were quite firm that I should get rid of her at once. This, I have no doubt, was kindly meant and excellent advice, with the one slight drawback that no-one would give her a home. Zoos that I telephoned were quite definite about this—Zoos, once they had established that she was a sloth-bear, said they did not like sloth-bears, I suppose because they have no tricks, nor very much charm (until you know them well), and unfortunately, with their long, shaggy dull coats they really look like nothing so much as an animated hearth rug.

However, I did learn from these discouraging telephone conversations that I was in possession of Melursus Ursinus, native only of India and Ceylon, that she was insectivorous, rather than carnivorous, and that her long, ugly nose, with its mobile lips, was for sucking up ants, and the frightening claws were for tearing the hard-baked termite mounds to pieces. For good measure, I was informed that she would be ill-tempered, undisciplined, and treacherous. Altogether she was not made to sound a particularly nice companion. So I took another long hard look at Melursus Ursinus, and she looked right back at me with her funny revolving pig eyes, which were crafty, a little bit

wicked, and very blind. Right then I think we both decided to
the Devil with all the good advice, and that we should just have
to make the best of one another, she to restrain her impressive
armament, and me to use my brains to try to find out what
would make her happy.

10

Meetings and Partings

On the morning after Bear's arrival I fetched Susie from her cage in the animal room. She jumped into my arms and we went upstairs to my bedroom. There, crawling about the floor, was Bear, newly arrived and displaying her huge head and small behind. Susie held on to me tightly, and stared at her in wide-eyed disbelief. Bear was scrabbling about the floor uncertainly, saying 'uh-uh' to herself, as she bumped into uncompromising pieces of furniture. What she really wanted to do was climb up on to my bed again, where it was safe and warm and cosy, but fortunately she was not yet strong enough to make the height.

'Down, Susie,' I said, relaxing my hold on her. 'Here's a playmate for you. Your very own Teddy Bear.' I might have added nightmare Teddy Bear, and maybe Susie thought just that, for she studied my face anxiously, as if seeking an answer there to the grotesque apparition that had suddenly joined the family. I tried to make her get down on the floor to join Bear, but she resisted furiously, and then, in that remarkable way that all animals, wild or domestic, have in sensing that appealing persuasion usually works much better than force in argument with human beings, she hid her face against my neck imploringly. The trick worked, just as she knew it would. I looked down at the incredibly scrubby and rather bald Bear, who was squinting up at Susie in equal astonishment, but with rather more enthusiasm than Sue had vouchsafed. So used did I become to Bear, with her silky grey muzzle, and long black coat, shining with health, that it was only when seeing an old television film of her again the other day, that I remembered back to what a really miserable specimen she had been when she and Sue were introduced.

This television film was short and made by Anglia Television of Susie, with Bear and dogs as supporting cast. It was not a very good film, because far too much time was taken up with me in close-up, looking my usual ninety, talking rather a lot of nonsense much too loudly. And considering the amount of work everyone put in, there were far too few shots of the animals, especially as any chimpanzee is a photographic natural.

A team of some dozen people arrived at eleven o'clock one morning. We were at it, with a short break for lunch, until seven in the evening, by which time I was ready, as the saying goes, to drop, having hauled that devastatingly weighty piece of monkey-flesh around the entire garden. We finally ended up in the house with the director asking me to run down the stairs in front of Susie. I had just about had my running for that day, but was willing to try the impossible—impossible, because how on earth could one run down the stairs more quickly than an ape? So we scrubbed that one, but we did get some quite good shots of Bear and Susie playing with a football in the hall—at least Susie played with the ball, and Bear tried to play with Susie. Suddenly, vastly to my surprise, as she had not done this before, Susie rolled over on her back and balancing the ball on her feet, spun it as professionally as any circus chimp, but, unfortunately, this was not filmed. That night Susie led the way into her cage thankfully, and when I looked in half an hour later there was no sign of her, but a gentle snoring floated out of her bed box.

I had very much hoped that Bear and Susie would like to live together in the animal room, not then knowing, naturally, the grotesque size to which Bear intended to grow. This was entirely for Susie's sake, to try to alleviate her loneliness when I was not at home. But Bear liked the dogs and she liked living with the dogs, and that was that.

As Susie grew older her character changed entirely. She seemed to lose a great deal of her gaiety and spontaneity: to become moody and broody, and her funny gargoyle face began to set in heavier lines, and to take on a slant of melancholy that

Just behind Bear is the cage at the back of the stable which we had to make to protect her from Bruce the labrador.

Ants! Bear is actually using her long claws to dig up a well-laid gravel drive. Two or three quick swipes and over an hour's repair work!

was disturbing when one looked for her to be alert and curious and full of fun. And gradually, markedly, I became less and less the mother figure. There were times when she would ignore my outstretched arms, when 'I'm going, Susie' would leave her cold, so that as her happiness dwindled, so did her obedience. I didn't worry much about the obedience, but her happiness was cause for grave concern. Before, she had always seemed to be smiling—now her face set heavily, and her eyes were sombre.

I suppose it didn't take a genius to realise that what she needed was more of her own kind, not necessarily a mate, because she was still very young, but fellow chimps to play with and to scrap with, and for all I know to talk to. I had been able to give her a great deal of affection, complete security, so necessary to uprooted wild animals, and plenty of delicious food. But still she was the only animal I have ever felt that I held as a prisoner.

Not that she showed the slightest sign of becoming savage, as I had been told she would. She was in superb physical condition—only the inner happiness was missing. She definitely did not like the outdoor life, and the thought of yet another long winter for her, when she would have to spend dismal hours alone in her cage when I was away, depressed me, and brought me round to thinking seriously of her future. Unbelievably, it began to be borne in upon me that I must find another home for her. Parting with an animal that has been a constant companion is a desperate heartbreak: one must forget the loving arms round one's neck, the screams of joy as one opens the cage, the contented puffing and other gentle noises as one is followed round the house. Yes, one must forget all that. What one is not entitled to forget is the life and future happiness of the animal with which one has been entrusted.

There are, indeed, only two things in the balance of such a decision: the greatest care not to betray this trust, and a complete conviction of gaining greater lasting happiness. On the one hand, with us she was much loved and completely safe, but she could also be lonely. In a new home she would inevitably miss us, and all major moves for wild animals are deeply disturbing; but if I felt I could find her a loving home, with the sort of individual attention she needed, the maximum liberty, and above all, companionship of her own age, that I would feel in duty bound to accept for her. Placing tamed wild animals is infinitely difficult, for Zoos do not want them—something people learn with alarm and surprise. People buy the poor creatures when they are little, helpless and cuddly, and when this extremely fleeting phase is over, confidently expect the nearest Zoo to take them. And the nearest Zoo very seldom does so.

But Susie and I were in luck. There is a very nice small Zoo in Yorkshire, and there were just three chimps there, and one a perfect boy friend for my growing girl. So the desperate decision was made, and I could only fervently hope that I had made the right one. Another world would open up for Susie, and a world that included her own kind. We had given her a splendid start to life, but she had outgrown us, and was ready for a change.

I funked the parting. I fled to London for a week, and tried not to think of the empty silent cage that would be waiting for me in the animal room, full of warm and poignant memories. Susie's departure would leave a big gap—she was something very special and quite apart—and the house would feel empty for a while, flat and dull. But I don't think I want another baby chimp, they twist themselves around you too much and tug at your emotions; and any living one of them would find its way into a tougher heart than mine.

11

Getting to Know Bear

Having established that Bear liked the dogs, and the dogs liked Bear, life became a little easier. By this time, of course, her name was firmly registered as Bear—there is really nothing very fancy you can do about an animal as plain as that. I suppose bears are, in fact, members of the dog family, and she was quite convinced that she was one, and whatever the dogs did, in her own bumbling way she copied.

My old yellow labrador Binna, who has mothered everything from a month old pig to a wallaby, by way of monkeys, owls and rats, came into her own again. Bear loved Binna; she was warm and solid and secure, and took a gentle interest in all the strange antics of the hideous little beast. Binna had a daughter who was a good deal less maternal, but who had the quiet tolerance of all good gundogs, and I put the three of them in one of the outside kennels.

Bear had not yet developed her awkward knack of climbing, so the outdoor run was a happy playground for her then. In those days she was just a novelty, a tiny joke that everyone was dying to see and to play with. Alas, because of her size, almost everyone became scared of her, although right to the end she was only a great clumsy, thoroughly good-natured, if somewhat unusual, animal; however, I can quite see that she could have been somewhat alarming to strangers.

The early days sped by. We found that, insectivorous or not, she ate everything: dog biscuits, chicken carcasses, apples, the entire contents of a dustbin if she got the chance. And milk. Rolling her button eyes ecstatically she would suck up just as much as she could get, and always held the milk bottle in the

79

palms of her hands. Thus she began slowly, slowly, slowly to fill out behind.

As with all my animals, her great joy was to get into the house. In those days she did no harm at all, and she was always clean. She liked to gallumph upstairs, and amble along to my bedroom, which she still remembered from her early hours with me, and climb on to the bed. One day I found her ensconced there, busily sucking a front paw, or front bunch of claws. She accompanied this exercise with a sewing-machine hum that I thought denoted a malaise that needed attention: perhaps a thorn in the pad, or a small cut. I took the paw out of her mouth, and started inspection. She snatched it back.

'Oh don't be silly, Bear,' I said. 'We'll soon see what the trouble is.' She snatched it back again. This abortive performance went on for some time, and the more often she snatched it back the more furiously she sucked, and the louder she hummed. I began to get worried—a thorn in a paw can go septic all too quickly; and if she wasn't going to let me look at it, anyone else who tried was going to have a pretty thin time. I talked to her in exactly the same idiotic way that Alice in Wonderland used for her white kitten.

'Now, Bear, you must let me have a *look*. I won't hurt. We'll just see what it is, and then we'll get some nice hot water and peroxide and bathe it, and it'll feel much better.'

If I had taken a good hard look at that pig-eye of hers, I might have given up the unequal struggle sooner. Bear intended to suck her paw, and she was jolly well going to do so, however long and bitter the fight.

When I look back on that paw-sucking incident now, it is with the greatest possible amusement. Just how silly can you get? But then again, how on earth was I to know? Paw-sucking and the accompanying hum is the sloth-bear's ultimate expression of contentment. When all is well with them they will do it by the hour, and when you know this, it is a charming and somehow very comforting sound. With my bear at least, it was also used as a graceful greeting, as graceful, anyhow, as a great shaggy animal could get. I found it extremely touching.

Just having my eyes cleaned up.
Bear didn't tolerate the dogs too close when she was eating.

When I arrived to take her for a walk she was absolutely over-
joyed, leaping up against the wire and calling out in her own
extraordinary language. But she also found time to snatch up her
paw and suck and hum, just to show how delighted she was. It
was very difficult to do all this at once, especially as there must
have been a tiny fear that I might not after all take her for a
walk; but then wild animals are amazingly polite: as with the
lion in its wild state, when every member of the pride, however
hungry, must make its greeting in correct order of seniority
before falling upon the kill, so Bear would always suck a paw
to me.

Downstairs she had her favourite armchair, which gives me
the haunting belief that the tale of the Three Bears was something
more than pure imagination. I truly regret that her final and
very satisfactory growth made it impossible for her to come
in the house any more, because it was fun to see her curled up
in her chosen chair, humming away so happily; but she really
became very heavy, and Sheraton tables did not exactly thrive
on constant contact with her.

12

A Case of Mistaken Identity

Not for long was Susie's cage in the animal room forlorn and empty. Soon there came an appeal from the R.S.P.C.A. to find a home for an African Green Monkey. It appeared that it belonged and was deeply attached to a boy, whose family were forced to move house and where they were going, no animals were allowed. The old, old story once again.

I hadn't really wanted another monkey, but it was a sad tale (aren't they all?) so I agreed to have him. I was not at home when the R.S.P.C.A. brought him over, complete with owner, since no-one else dared touch him. When I rang up eagerly to find out what he was like, the reports were dubious. His owner, it seemed, had been able to do anything with him, and the two were touchingly devoted. But this devotion was not showing any sign of rubbing off on anyone else, and he was being left strictly alone until I returned.

When I got home, I went straight to the animal room, in high excitement. And there, sitting in Susie's cage, was a medium-sized grey-green monkey, with one of the most evil expressions I have ever seen on an animal face. 'Heavens!' I thought, 'what have you let yourself in for here?' He had two great molar teeth permanently exposed, so that the poor beast could not have looked very amiable even if he wished, but his opaque monkey eyes held something beyond opaqueness—a kind of primordial savagery, or awareness, that was frightening. 'Poor Bimbo,' I crooned to him. 'Poor boy then.' I might as well have crooned to one of Epstein's nastier nightmares for all the change of expression I was awarded. So I called Peter, our gardener, into consultation. What should we do with this rather unpleasant new member of our circle?

All that had so far been done to Bimbo was to feed him—cleaning had been left strictly in abeyance. Apparently he had never been handled by anyone other than his owner, and had a reputation for considerable savagery. This, with a monkey, puts one in no mean spot—how to find out if it is so or not, without risking a really dangerous bite? None of us just then felt much like playing the guinea-pig game—not even me, because I have a sixth, seventh, or even eighth sense about animals, and, right at that moment, there was absolutely no feeling of warmth between us at all.

At this time I had the usual crowd of dogs (some of them mine, some of them orphans), two tiny marmosets, Bear, my present white rat, Tatty-puss, and a very dull animal fairly rare in this country—an American opossum. Dull, did I say? Well, that was what I thought then, but one can always learn.

Possie, as we called this strange creature, looked a little like a bush-baby—she had the same pink knobbly hands—a little like a marten and a little like a rat. That is to say her tail ended up like a rat's, but was covered with fur to a third of the way down, and this tail was prehensile. She had the most wonderful dense soft coat of a reddish brown colour: that, indeed, was the only beautiful thing about her, because otherwise she verged on the revolting. She had an extraordinary way of walking, belly to floor, with the short legs so manipulated that she progressed with a Monroe wiggle. She had flat, reddish eyes, and a pink nose like a pig. She was quite gentle with me, but nothing very much seemed to penetrate, perhaps because she was a true nocturnal, and any disturbance during the day merely annoyed her. I kept her in my bathroom, where she slept like a dormouse, dawn to dusk, on top of the splash curtain round my bath. Around six o'clock she would descend head first down the curtain, tail at the ready to hook itself round anything convenient, to look for her supper. She liked all sorts of things, fruit and nuts, eggs and cake, and of course, milk. After this, if I had left my cupboard door open, which was an almost certain bet, she would creep in there, curl up amongst my

underclothes, and go to sleep once more. She was the sleepiest
creature I had ever known. Well, that was Possie.

But to return to Bimbo, the same routine was adhered to for
something like a week. He was fed regularly, but nobody
touched him. I used to go in every day to talk to him, and he
would stare back at me steadily, without a change in that
monstrous expression. But one day I was brushing Pekaboo on
the table in the animal room, a long and dreary battle against
burrs and brambles and wet mats (shades of show pekes on
their satin cushions!) when I noticed that Bimbo was tugging
at the strap and chain that was still attached to his middle, as
it had been when he arrived. Previously he had been too busy
keeping up his hostile stare to let us see that he was uncomfor-
table, but now, when I approached the cage, he gave me a
worried, not an angry look, and continued to tear at the leather
round his waist. To my great concern I saw that underneath the
collar was a deep flesh wound, where the too tight strap had
grown into him. When he let go the leather with his hand, it
slipped back into the raw red gash again and covered it up
completely. But it hurt. It must have hurt like hell, so he pulled
it out of the wound again, and tried to wrench it off. Of course,
poor monkey, he hadn't a hope, and presently he let it slide
back into its torturing groove, closed his eyes for a minute,
and rocked back and forth a while.

I didn't know what to do. The mildest animal would go
berserk if one started messing about with an open sore like
that, and he was not the mildest animal. I went on brushing, or
tearing at, Pekaboo for a bit, but Bimbo started wrenching at
his strap again and I couldn't bear it, so I went away to think
over what should be done. There seemed only one answer, and
that was to get Mr Sutherland to chloroform him, and to cut
the collar off as quickly as possible while he was asleep. What
happened afterwards was uninteresting for the moment; the
great thing was to stop the present torture.

That night I went to the animal room again. The little
marmosets were curled up asleep in their woolly blanket, but
Bimbo, whom I thought should also be asleep, was staring out

...r really enjoyed playing
...h her favourite pole;
...haps a natural instinct.

Salute!

This was the day that Bear was temporarily stranded.

sombrely at nothing in particular. He swung round as I came in, and the look he gave me was quite other than the deep hostile scowl that I so mistrusted. It almost seemed that, as he had shared his pain with me, we were on another footing, perhaps not friends quite, but at least not enemies.

I started to talk gently to him, but almost at once he began his agonising strap-tearing again. I stared helplessly at him. How on earth, I asked myself angrily, could his owner, who loved him and could do anything with him, leave him like that? Quite without thinking, in my frustration, I put two fingers through the wire. In an instant Bimbo was over against the wire and had clasped my fingers in his long strong hands. Holding my fingers in a strangle grip—I suppose he could have made a fair play at biting them off had he so wished—he gazed intently into my face. I forgot all about my fingers, so fascinated was I in the change of expression I saw there. How on earth, I wondered, *does* a monkey change its expression? The mask-like face remained the same, and yet its whole aspect underwent complete metamorphosis. The eyes remained the same and yet the evil seemed to have gone from them, the terrible teeth hung down, but they looked to me now without menace, the beetling brows still beetled, and yet this could now be taken for worry and not for threat.

While all this was going through my mind, he still had my fingers, now tucked against his chest. I tried to pull them away gently, but the grip hardened. And suddenly something seemed to explode inside me, and I said to myself, in my most scathing and condemnatory vein, 'Ha! you're supposed to love animals, and yet you stand here while this poor monkey suffers torture with every movement. Yes, you stand here sobbing your heart out over his pain, and you do sweet Fanny Adams about it, because you're frightened of him. Scared stiff of an animal not a quarter your size. An animal who has no-one to turn to for help except you. Struck lucky, hasn't he? So he bites you, so what? It won't be the first time and it won't be the last. If you go to bed tonight without attempting to do something to ease this creature's pain, I won't be shipmates with you any longer, so get cracking.' I can be pretty tough with myself at times, and it mostly works. It had to work that night.

'Bimbo,' I said, gently but firmly. 'Let go of my fingers and I'll see what I can do about that bloody strap. I won't be long, but I must rustle up a sharp pair of scissors.'

He may have understood, or he may not have, but after a moment or so, he released my hand, and climbed wearily back on to his bar. I went in search of the scissors.

I'm not really frightened of animals and once I had decided to get that strap off, I forgot all about the risk. I flung the cage door wide and called to him, and strap or no strap, in one colossal bound, he was on my shoulder, had wrapped his arms round my neck and buried his face against me. Poor monkey.

He was quiet enough and I still had my ear intact, but the grip, by which he held on to me, was somewhat strangulating. And just as with Susie, if I tried to remove it, it tightened a hundredfold. The sharp scissors hung useless in my hand, and I was rather at a loss for the next move. Then suddenly I thought that the collar round his middle was a strap with a buckle, and loathsomely tight though it was, perhaps I could undo that buckle, very gently.

I went over to the table and jettisoned the scissors, then quietly and carefully raised my hand to the lump of dynamite on my shoulder. Steadily, firmly, I felt through the thick fur in search of the buckle. I found it, fortunately almost in the middle of his back. Gritting my teeth against the thought of the raw flesh that I couldn't help scraping, I started to work the buckle loose. Bimbo continued to strangle me, but he made no protest until I had the buckle quite undone, when the weight of the attached chain dragged the collar off him; and then he gave a convulsive shudder and banged his head against mine in a final spasm of pain.

But it was off! I could hardly believe, as I wiped the heavy sweat off my forehead, that the whole thing had been so quick and easy, and I felt a surge of triumphant satisfaction. Had I been less triumphant and less satisfied, and had I put Bimbo back in his cage with love and a nice supper, I should have side-stepped the disaster that was now lying in wait for me. But I was determined to show him off to my aunt, who not surprisingly, found him completely terrifying. So walking carefully with my precious load, who I thought must still be pretty sore, I went upstairs. I called to my aunt, who ran along the landing, then stopped, petrified. 'If I hadn't seen this with my own eyes,' she said, 'I wouldn't have believed it.' So, with a superior smile, I swept on to my bedroom.

I wasn't going to be superior very long though. Bimbo was holding on to me more loosely now, but he was heavy. So I sat us both on the bed. Had this been a film—and it would have rated a horror-comic—this would have been the moment for warning music. Because, when I flumped myself down on the bed, I sat hard on the unfortunate opossum, who had come through the ever-open door, and was once more curled up asleep.

As ever, with my animals, the unpredictable happened. There was I, worrying slightly about the African Green savage sitting on my shoulder, when out from under the eiderdown came a tornado of red fur, pink hands and very adequate white teeth. Bimbo had slipped down on to my lap, and Possie went for his throat like a dart to a double. With his fierce reputation one would have thought that Bimbo would have been quite a match for this little fury, but he seemed stunned.

A sudden horrible warning flashed through my brain that someone had said that an opossum is a deadly foe that hangs on relentlessly to the end. Just as Possie was about to sink her teeth into Bimbo's throat, I grabbed her by the tail. I hadn't remembered that it was a prehensile tail, but I think I should have done it just the same. Back came the enraged little animal against my face, and bit hard into my cheek. But, by an act of grace, she realised her mistake, and doubled back at Bimbo again. The stupid monkey hadn't moved. 'For Heaven's sake —get!' I yelled at him, grabbing Possie again (one never learns). This time, maddened by the rough grasp on her prehensile tail, Possie sank her teeth into my thigh. This gave me time to fling Bimbo off my lap, and to swing Possie, who had again swiftly released me, into the bathroom, and to bang the door on that extremely bloody battle. Bloody for me that was: neither of the animals was even scratched. Blood was pouring from my leg. But such is my reaction to these catastrophies that I just couldn't stop laughing—I tottered down to my aunt with Bimbo on my shoulder, still pouring blood, and was most surprised that she didn't find it cryingly funny too. Of course, my face, which hardly bled at all, was a terrible mess in the morning and for some weeks later, and I still carry two rather ageing scars. But it might have been worse. And that's the way things turn out with my sort of animal-keeping; I had been commendably careful over the African Green monkey, only to sit both of us down on the far more savage American opossum.

But alas, Bimbo could not settle into our family group. He developed an embarrassing passion for me that was quite un-restrainable, and apart from this, he was dangerous to anyone else—that first evil look on his face had been no illusion. One day, when he was on my shoulder, I opened the schoolroom door, where Steve and his tutor were working. With a speed that left me no time to do anything at all, Bimbo was over the table, had plunged his fangs into the tutor's hand and had returned to my shoulder in one big bound. It was a bad bite: Mr Oliviera had to pay several visits to the doctor, the doctor who has so far been spared my bites and gashes, as I heal up with the same ease as the animals that occasionally inflict them.

Fortunately Flamingo Park was willing to give a home to Bimbo, so he followed Susie up to that very pleasant Zoo.

Galago Maholi. No
bigger than a woman's
hand.

Well bless my soul! You
are a long way down
there.

I could have sworn that I heard the distinctive 'click' of a camera.

13

The Photographers

It was not long before one or two people heard that I had a strange bear. I don't believe that anyone had had what you might vaguely describe as a 'pet' sloth-bear in this country before—I suppose they don't exactly lend themselves to that role because they are so cumbersome. Anyway, the rumour got around and the photographers started to arrive.

It was extremely funny to watch their relative reactions, for frankly, many of them were terrified. One poor man, indeed, was so scared that he literally turned green in the face, and I mean, literally. I was so fascinated watching him, that I failed to watch Bear, who was in a playful mood, and I soon found myself flat on my back. The way Bear used to throw you was to grab you round the ankles with her rounded claws and butt you with her large head. Therefore the only place you could go was straight over backwards. This photographer wasn't sure whether to bolt for it, or whether to take a picture of this extremely undignified scene. Unfortunately he decided on the picture.

But the first of the great photographers to arrive was Robert Chandler, Picture Editor of the *News of the World*. It would be ridiculous to suggest that I make a double harness act with the *News of the World*, but the R.S.P.C.A. wanted to give a boost to a Charity matinée I had arranged for them of *The Bluebird*, at the Lyric, Hammersmith. The Belgian Ambassador and Donald Campbell had very kindly consented to come, and we were starry-eyed for any publicity we could get.

Robert Chandler is a remarkable man. I should think I know pretty well all about photographers by now, but I was innocent back in those days. Now I know the photographers who rush hither and yon, who leap up on walls, shouting, who always have the wrong instrument clasped to their pullovers and who are always running out of film. I know the superior ones, whose armour tended to crack during the first interview with Bear. I know the nice gentle ones, the sour boned ones, and the fresh, ambitious ones. But Mr Chandler came under none of these headings. He was very quiet and reserved, with a mild sense of humour, and a battered old plate camera, that, in my ignorance, horrified me to bits.

Mr Chandler hurried not at all, neither did Bear worry him, though, indeed, she was not very big in those days. I was convinced that he had missed every good pose and angle and my exasperation mounted. I even hastened him over his luncheon, most discourteously, because I was convinced he had not had a decent shot all day and I was determined that he should! (I was still under the influence of the wall-jumpers.) He remained quite unruffled. I was even convinced that he had not taken in enough about Bear to write adequate captions, so just as he was leaving I thrust an article into his hand.

'This is a copy of an article I've written,' I said. 'It might help to read it.'

When no pictures, not one, appeared in the *News of the World* next day, I said to my aunt, 'There, you see! Just nothing came out!'

It was not until a week or so later that I received from Mr Chandler a set of the most excellent photographs, some of which appear in this book. And it was not until much, much later that we suddenly discovered that 'my article' had got itself printed in *Animal Life*, which is run by the *News of the World*! So much for my views on the vague Mr Chandler.

The next photographer was Ida Kar, who was taking pictures for the magazine, *Animals*.

Ida took the whole thing very seriously indeed, even staying the night and belting on with the camera work next day. She wasn't in the least frightened of Bear; in fact her assistant took a delightful photograph of Bear standing up against Ida's back while Ida herself was photographing another animal.

We all got on famously together and were having a merry time when suddenly disaster struck: Bear found a two gallon drum of paraffin. I am sorry to relate that Bear was distinctly alcoholic, and this find of paraffin enchanted her. Clutching the tin with her claws she drank greedily and when it fell over, she continued to lap it up with enthusiasm on the ground, I was horrified. There was simply nothing I could do to stop her, because she was a very strong-minded lady, as well as a peculiarly hefty one physically. So she finished her paraffin.

For my part, I rushed to the telephone to contact our excellent vet and when I had him on the line, I babbled incoherently that I was sure Bear had taken such a quantity, that she would certainly die of it, and could he come at once with a stomach pump, etc., etc. He listened to all this nonsense with commendable patience, and then explained, gently, that paraffin was really not injurious, certainly not fatal; and if it happened to give her a bit of tummy-ache she should have some raw eggs and milk.

Well, it did give her a goodly tummy-ache, and as ever, when she was ill or frightened she rushed to me for comfort. When she was really ill I *could* comfort her, because she became pathetically gentle and droopy. I took her into the house, and sitting with her on the sofa, I held her in my arms while I rubbed her tummy. She took a very good view of this, and Ida took some more photographs. When I thought Bear was sufficiently eased, I went to mix the eggs and milk, and that, as far as we were concerned, was the end of the day for Bear. Mr Sutherland the vet was perfectly correct: next day Bear was her happy, vastly energetic self again and we continued to photograph.

In a way Ida was very fortunate because it was in the middle of that hideous winter of 62/63, when the land was turned into iron and covered with a vast blanket of snow. This meant that Bear could go all round the garden, and pose against the pretty background of the house without being able to do a mite's worth of damage with her tiresome claws. When later photographers came, they were very disappointed to have to make do with a roam around the farm, but if Bear got on to a nice, soft, green lawn, she was through to Australia in ten seconds flat. It was bad enough for poor Peter to have to look after a bear, but to have his beautifully kept garden disembowelled as well would have been just a bit too steep.

The next well-known photographer to arrive was John Simmons, who came with charming Valerie Jackson from a woman's magazine. They lunched with me and I was able to explain a little of bear psychology—this I had learned was helpful, as it was really not quite fair to pitch a photographer straight out into a field with a bear rampant, and Bear on her day could ramp.

Neither of these two, perhaps because of all my earnest explanation, was in the least bit alarmed by Bear. And we went about photographing her the right and only way, which was to go for a long walk with her so that she settled down. John Simmons had a zoom lens, and he took some of the finest pictures of her that I have. He was also really very brave, because Bear thought at first that the zoom lens was a gun and she registered a sincere and vivid protest; however, all was well in the end, as soon as she realised that no harm was intended, and John actually went down on his hands and knees a few inches from her nose and took superlative pictures. This made me madly nervous as I never *knew* what Bear was going to do, and one is not exactly in a defensive position when one is crawling about on the ground. However, Bear took absolutely no notice whatsoever.

Having completed our mission we started for home. What suddenly struck Bear I shall never know, but with a festive cry she tore off into the bushes, and the next moment was seen to be climbing wildly up a vast willow tree. Bear had climbed little trees before, but not often, and this sudden ascent of Everest was, and still is, a mystery to me.

Of course she got stuck up there, because she was never much of a climber, and she must simply have been showing off. I was very worried about her because she kept on trying to descend backwards into thin air, but some instinct for self-preservation stopped her, and she would turn around and stare

Really! My mouth is positively watering.

Sometimes Bear ate things which she shouldn't and they had to be extracted.

unhappily down at us. David, our garden boy, tried to climb up to get her, but it was an awkward sort of tree, and I don't quite know what he would have done, if he had been able to reach her. Finally, he fetched our longest ladder, propped it against the tree, and we left her to it; as I knew that as long as we were prepared to baby-sit she would happily play the baby. And I was right. Some five minutes later, puffing with anxiety and excitement she rejoined us, and was then quite ready for the bread and milk waiting for her in her house.

Shortly after this happy day with the cameras, Alan Robertson came to stay. He drops in from time to time to photograph my animals, purely under the old pals act. And most successfully too. I hadn't seen all John Simmons' photographs by then, and was very anxious to get some more of Bear. I knew Alan had always been pretty anti-Bear—in fact he had told my husband long, long ago that she should be got rid of immediately. It didn't make me like him any the less—I just thought he was a bit mixed up, or had bear-allergy or something.

Anyway, I said brightly that we would take Bear for a walk. As she came charging out of her house, he let out a yelp. She had doubled in size since he had seen her last and he was horrified. And as luck would have it she was in a skittish mood. As the corn was standing high, we had to turn up the hill and Bear turned too and held out her arms. She looked enormous weaving there above us.

'You're absolutely raving!' yelled Alan.

'Get down, Bear, and don't be silly,' I said, as usual. Bear flumped down (as usual) and ambled away up the hill. Alan joined me looking rather miserable. Bear-walking wasn't one of his favourite pastimes it seemed. Presently we negotiated a cart-track, walking in the ruts. Alan looked round and said with alarm: 'Heavens—she's in the same track as me!'

I couldn't help laughing. 'She won't hurt you, I promise,' I said. 'She's perfectly quiet and gentle. Just keep walking.' Finally we went up a green lane, where the trees had delicious leaves. These are the leaves that Bear is eating in the cover photograph—and Alan took the picture.

When we were home again I had the idea that it would be fun to have a picture of Bear following my horse Diabolo, and Alan thought so too. So I flung a stride saddle on that amiable horse, and crossing a little bridge over the stream, closely followed by Bear, we went into the paddock where Steve's pony and an unbroken yearling pony colt were turned out. The pandemonium that ensued is well-nigh indescribable. The yearling first rushed at Bear, who fled in terror, not being very brave; then it flew at me in an attempt to bite my knee, then rushed back at Bear and tried to kick her; then flew at Diabolo and tried to kick *him* (as my knee by this time was safely out of the way). Altogether a most friendly character: he remained in the family for only another week. As the noise died down Bear was found to have disappeared completely, so shouting at the unpleasant yearling to keep out of my way, I left the paddock in search of her.

Poor Bear was standing on the other side of the bridge, looking very forlorn. She never did understand it when anyone was unkind to her, and she had certainly done no harm to that beastly pony. I tried to make her follow Diabolo up her usual cart-track, but she was thoroughly upset and for the only time in her life she went into hiding in the bushes. After a while, I got worried, and stabling Diabolo, went in search of her. I could find her nowhere. I went back to the stable, where Alan was waiting patiently. 'I'm worried,' I said. 'She has never done this before.' Suddenly Alan smiled and pointed. 'Look,' he said, 'something for you!' and there round the corner of the stable block came a hunched dejected figure, very slowly, very sadly—and straight to me for comfort.

'You old silly!' I said as I stroked her. 'You weren't even hurt. What a fuss!' and I led her back to her cage and her comforting bread and milk.

Being insatiable for pictures of Bear, and always hopeful that we would get unusual ones by chance, there are many other people who have come to our home, either arming themselves with their own cameras, or with ones supplied by me. Alan Robertson was not the only one to get in a rut with Bear!

When Gordon Fairley first came to discuss publication of this book he did much the same and muttered equally mirthless noises. On one occasion we were just taking Bear out. Since she was more than usually thirsty, she made a rush for the corrugated iron rain butt, close to which he happened to be standing. He was, I think, delighted that he was out of Bear's visual range and that she was thirsty. I doubt if Bear even saw him. The ant-sucking snout, drawing up water, happily drowned comment.

It was on this day that Bear found an ants' nest in the drive and we got a good picture of her actually eating the very small and insignificant English ants. She took up quite a large section of the gravel drive in a very few sweeps of those claws specially evolved for just such use.

Some of the other photographs in this book were taken by amateurs and I am grateful to them and to the professionals for all the time and patience which they expended.

14

Walks—and Rides

After she had been denied the house because she was getting so big, the daily walk was the highlight of Bear's life. She was insatiably curious, and each fresh smell or sound had her huffing and puffing with delight.

We ambled slowly around the grounds, finding delicious pieces of rotted wood and little mounds of earth, and even a stray ant or two. One day we walked up the green lane at the back of the house, where three immense old willow boles lie rotting. Here was Paradise indeed! Bear scrambled up on to the nearest one, and started to rip off the bark with her powerful claws, and with what delight she discovered the creepy crawlies huddled underneath. I was almost as excited as she—'There, silly!' I shouted, as a whole bunch scuttered off while her back was turned. But she didn't like woodlice. I suppose a woodlouse is not a termite, though I have forgotten to check this. But she would have stayed there excavating happily for as long as my patience held out, which was not too long. Indeed I felt like a nurse in the park watching children at play. The only thing was that I had no bench, no knitting, no nothing at all, so we soon moved on. The moment I started off, Bear left all her treasures and rushed after me—Melursus Ursinus had no intention of being left behind.

There was a very curious thing about this bear—following. As she grew older she would let me get further away from her— indeed the whole length of a long field, if she had found a very special earth mound. She had very little sense of smell, and was near-sighted—by far her most acute sense was that of hearing. But the fascinating part of this contact between us was that the moment I got behind something solid—a wall, even a belt of

Quite often Bear showed delight by making this grimace.

This picture shows those long claws.

trees, she knew at once. Recently she could keep tags on me more easily, but when she was younger at once her head would come up, the elephant ears would come forward, and with an agonised 'Oo-er—Oo-er' she would come charging in the direction she knew me to have taken. Sometimes she would almost go past, when a sudden scent would halt her, and grunting irritably, as much as to say, 'She might at least have told me!' she would fall in with the dogs again. But what was it, I wonder, that told her she was no longer in direct line to me? Scent, certainly not. Sight, likewise. Indeed, it is the blindness of the wild sloth-bear that makes it so dangerous. It will charge any strange object outside its range of vision, a range that is probably not more than 10 yards. No, I think it is a wave, a sound wave if you will—that is cut off the moment one gets behind a solid object. No doubt someone will be able to tell me this is nonsense, but I can think of no other explanation.

At that time it was warm enough for Susie to come out with us, although, as I have already said, this was far from her favourite pastime. The only thing she did enjoy was bully-ragging Bear. With her terrifying steel fingers she would grasp a shaggy black ear, and start off across the lawn with Bear lumbering in her wake. Suddenly she would go into reverse, and flinging herself across unfortunate Bear, would yank her over on to her back, where she would lie meekly, surprised grey tummy upwards. But oddly enough she in no way resented it, and took it as all in the day's walk.

One day we thought it might be the thing if Bear went for a swim. I had it firmly fixed in what I term my mind that bears like water. So we inveigled her to the edge of the pond, and with a deft shove, landed her in. She loathed it. We soon hauled her out, and had to laugh heartily, because, just like a pekingese, she was all fur and precious little body; and with that enormous head, she had gone into the water as Bear and emerged as definitely gargoyle. So that was the end of Bear's swimming. Like an old lady who carefully holds up her skirts to paddle, she loved playing in puddles, where she splashed the mud over her nose, and came out looking more grotesque than ever.

7

It was late autumn by this time, and we planned to have several small shoots over our ground. Although I work the gun-dogs I thought it would be fun to take Bear along just for the exercise. She thought so too. It was a lovely morning, and she trundled happily after us, amusing everybody vastly, because she was quite small and unfrightening still. Rather occupied with the dogs, though I can't think why, as we never have anything to shoot, in some extraordinary way I lost her, or I should say rather, she lost me. We were just lining up down by the stream, when I became aware of this horrible fact. I became agitated. Where on earth do you start looking for an animal that has never been more than a few inches from your heels? I was just asking myself this sixty-four-thousand dollar question, when happening to look way over on the hill where the cars were parked, I saw a pathetic little black form nosing about amongst them (Bear had the same feeling for cars as a 17 year old—if she had to swap me for something it would surely have been for a car). Between us and the cars lay a vast patch of high reed intersected by deep drainage ditches. Without thought, in my mother-hen relief, I let out a yell of hail and welcome. Up came Bear's head, forward came the old elephant ears, and with her usual 'Oo-er—Oo-er' she came belting for the bog.

I was absolutely horrified. I had several times fallen into the drainage ditches myself when driving birds and they were very wide and deep. As she disappeared into the reeds I could only go on calling and hoping, and the reeds rippled as she plunged on. I shall never know how she managed it without hurt, but, straight as a die, she came to me, grunting with pleasure and a breathless sense of achievement. As I bent to pull the broken rushes out of her rough coat I reflected that very few dogs would have faced that crossing, and she had not even hesitated. Altogether it was not a good day, for at the first sound of a gunshot she became completely panic-stricken, and I had to take her home. I was certain then, and am more than ever so now, that her mother had been shot. For sometime later, David, the garden boy, took her for a long, and I mean long, walk up to the wood, as he wanted to see how the harvest was getting on.

The men working the combine-harvester were a good deal less enthusiastic about seeing how Bear was getting on, and leaping on to their noisesome machine, started it up. At the very first bang, Bear let out an agonised roar, whipped round and made straight for home, her house, and safety. To me it was a very remarkable thing that a wild animal, and she was never anything else, when frightened to the point of panic, should rush back into what was nothing less than captivity. I should have thought it much more likely that she should have hidden in the woods, or even climbed a tree. But that flimsy cage of hers in the dog kennel was home, she knew it, she loved it and she was secure there.

However, this love of Bear for her cage has made me feel a little differently towards Zoos. Before I had her, frankly, they made me feel sick, if for any reason I had to go to one. Obviously there are Zoos and Zoos, and in the good ones some of the animals can surely be quite happy. I only wish that more was done, though, to amuse them. Bear had marrow bones twice a week and they kept her happy for hours. She also had a long thick log of wood for chewing, often replaced, on which she rocked. These seem very simple things to provide, matched against the enormous pleasure that they give a caged animal.

Being autumn we thought it would be fun to go blackberrying. Stephen collected the Land-Rover and I collected the dogs. Suddenly I thought—why not take Bear. It might be possible to get her into the Land-Rover. Stephen looked horrified when, along with the dogs, Bear lolloped up to the front door. She gave one look at the back of the Land-Rover, hitched her great claws over the tailboard, and with a grunt and a mighty heave she was in. Steve and I gazed at her in astonishment, so naturally and easily had she done it; and what made it even more grotesque was that I had to lift in one of the labradors. Bear sat down comfortably on a back seat and rolled her eyes. However, since I thought panic might strike when the engine started and the jolting began, I decided for the start to run behind.

Bear just loved it. She fell over the dogs and the dogs fell over

her and she thought it a splendid new game. In parentheses, one
of the sadder aspects of keeping such a playful but powerful
animal is that you *cannot* play with her. Several times she has
indeed rolled me on the ground, without even scratching me,
but it is exactly like being covered by a vast fur rug, which, to
add to the general gaiety, is playfully nipping you, though
certainly never enough to break the skin. Anyway, as things
were, I saw no future in this running business and quickly
called a halt. Bear eyed me suspiciously, preparatory to getting
out again, so I popped quickly into the cab.

Bear travelled beautifully. Every now and again a rubbery
nose would appear through a gap in the canvas by my hand,
and my young son, who was driving, would get a tremendous
bash in the back as Bear thought about coming through to join
us or became 'unseated' by the bumpiness of our farm tracks.
However, we arrived without incident, the dogs tumbled out,
and we went round to see what Bear would do. Bear was in no-
wise flustered. She reversed and descended carefully backwards
like a fat woman getting off a bus.

Of course blackberrying was made to measure for a fruit-
eating Bear. It was a sort of 'I'll take the high road and you
take the low road' as we reached up above, and she sucked
along behind us, between us, and before us. Bear was a happy
animal—she oozed a kind of quiet contentment that I, at
least, found very moving. Sometimes I think how little it took
to please her, and what a dull life she led when I was away:
and even when I was there we showed each other little affection, because of the very size of her. But when we were coming
home from a long walk sometimes, and she was rather tired, she
came very close against my legs, and I patted her rough back,
and sometimes she took my hand very gently in her mouth
and swung it a bit.

When we had filled our baskets—and very little blackberrying
is more than enough for me—Bear heaved herself into the back
of the Land-Rover again. But this time we had to stop to close a
gate, and Bear hastily re-descended. And instead of getting
into the back again when we got into the cab, this time she

appeared on the flat bonnet of the car. Slowly and with great dignity she climbed up on to the canvas roof, and there with a snort of satisfaction, she lay down. She was extremely pleased with her hammock, and we debated letting her ride there; but I was afraid she would get jolted off. Where it would bother no member of the cat family, Bear seems to be very stiff and inflexible and I was sure she would get hurt. She was quite willing to go into the back again, and it is one up on intelligence to her that she never again tried to climb on to the roof.

She nursed a not so secret passion for the Land-Rover. She was quite convinced that if she sucked the exhaust pipe for long enough something quite delectable would come out. When, quite obviously, it did not, she gave it a mighty wang with her forepaw, and climbed into the back to see if there were any sacks to play with. There nearly always were, and she swirled them around joyfully until one by one they flew out of the car. Tired of that, she then climbed into the cab and draped herself becomingly over the steering wheel.

At this time Binna and her daughter were both due to pup, so Bear was left alone in a loose-box with Bruce, my big and beautiful stud labrador. One day to my horror I heard a terrific commotion coming from the box. Running madly to save Bruce, as I thought, I was confronted by the most remarkable sight. Bear was lying flat on her back with Bruce standing over her in a position of extreme menace. When this happened a second time I had Bear's living quarters divided from the dogs. She had half the stable and they had the front part. I still wanted her to be with the dogs, so that she would never get that feeling of loneliness that leads on to fear.

The puppies duly arrived, and there was much coming and going in the outside kennels. Bear watched this thoughtfully. When the time came for them to be fed out in the runs, the thought had hatched. Slowly, deliberately she climbed over the high kennel grill, let herself carefully down backwards and proceeded to suck up the enticing food, while the terrified puppies cowered in the corner. But they were soon quite used to her, even to going in the Land-Rover with her. Bear never hurt any animal at all, but she was rather naughty once with one of the boys who used to look after her. John was 17 and devoted to animals in the carefree way of all boys. One day he had a piece of food in his hand which he offered to Bear, then he snatched it away again. Then offered it again. Ditto.

'John,' I warned, 'she'll bite you.' But John knew best. Or thought he did. Bear moved suddenly, swift as an adder and John stood up with two nicely bleeding fingers and a very white face.

'It serves you right,' I said crossly, because to see any animal teased makes me very angry. 'Now go indoors and get that disinfected and tied up,' I added, without a vestige of sympathy. But John was wonderful with Bear. He would play with her for hours, and he was always thinking of some new way to amuse her. He even tried to put a collar on her, which she loathed, and she would go tearing off up the lane for her exercise, with John flying faithful and breathless in her wake. I have an ambition to remove that silly tag 'Sloth', and to have these fascinating creatures re-named 'Beck's Bears', for Bear had proved the most interesting and charming wild animal I had ever owned.

The following story, though funny, once again shows, alas, my sad ignorance of animal habit.

Being delighted with Diabolo in the trap and deeply impressed with his jumping powers I began to have hazy dreams of hunting again, and hunting to me means a side-saddle. So one fine morning I buckled my faithful old saddle on to this vast vanner, who took it quite without surprise. What is surprising is that almost everyone thinks that horses should be frightened of a side-saddle—sensible animals, they much prefer you should hang on by your saddle rather than by their mouths. Having completed this feat it suddenly occurred to me that Bear might be prepared to follow too. While riding herd on the dogs I thought I could easily keep an eye on her as well. It was just a question of whether she would connect me with a disembodied voice from above!

I needn't have worried at all. She was absolutely delighted with the idea and might have been doing it all her life. So off we went, this strange cavalcade of three labradors, a whippet, a St Bernard and a bear.

It was a heavenly day and we were all delighted to be out, including my gross horse who did a few elephantine bucks. Probably because of the general pleasure, I scarcely noticed how far afield we were going, and presently we found ourselves right off our land and trotting along a side road.

Up till now Bear had been going like a steam-engine and I was just congratulating myself on this splendid way of exercising us all, when I suddenly realised she was no longer behind me. I hauled my war horse to a stand and let out my usual jovial shouts. Nothing. Much concerned, we retraced our steps. More nothing. Terrible visions of Bear having been run over assailed me, though goodness knows by what, or that she had left the desolate airfield we were on, for the nearest village. It only now occurred to me that she had never been off our property before. I seldom panic over anything but my animals, but I make up for it then in splendid measure. Hysteria was mounting nicely when there came a sound of rustling in the bushes by the side of the road. Leaping off—no, let's admit it, scrambling off, I hitched Diabolo to a convenient post and plunged bushwards. And there sat Bear, puffing away, and when she saw me she started her paw-hum act at once.

'Oh, come along, Bear, really,' I said crossly (I'm always very cross as panic subsides). 'What are you hanging about there for.' For incredible to relate it had not occurred to Your Dopiness that the animal was exhausted. I had always thought of Bear as swift and tireless—which over short distances indeed she was. My sort of bear-keeping naturally was a matter of trial and error—I know now that bears are really wanderers by nature, and although they can put on an alarming burst of pursuit speed they can by no means keep it up. So it was really rather wonderful that Bear had come so far so fast in the wake of her ignorant mistress; now she could go no more.

Well, that *was* a to-do. We were really a very long way from home, measured in bear-lugging miles. I could hardly get her up on Diabolo since I could scarcely get up there myself, and I certainly couldn't leave her. So I sat down beside her to think this out. She stretched out and laid her rough old head on my lap and puffed and blew: she was really completely done-up. Presently, however, she struggled to a sitting position and surveyed the scene. 'You old silly!' I said, but I knew she wasn't, and was just thankful she hadn't had a heart attack. Just at that moment I heard a car approaching. Struggling out of the bushes and over Bear, I rushed into the road. A surprised car ground to a halt. And well it might be surprised: Diabolo was straddled half over the tarmac, Louis, the St Bernard, was sound asleep right across it, the labradors were mooching, and here was a wild woman leaping out of the bushes, brandishing a stick. But I was so delighted to see a car on this lonely road that I didn't give the *mise-en-scène* a thought.

'Be a good Samaritan' I gasped. 'Stop at the nearest telephone box and ring my home number. Tell them my bear is exhausted and will they send the Land-Rover.' When the driver looked a little astonished, I repeated all this testily and with a perfunctory wave plunged back to Bear.

Bear by now was feeling much better and was on the amble again. So I collected my scattered family, and we began to walk back very slowly in the direction of home. We took it at a gentle wander with plenty of snuffling and sitting down, and presently the Land-Rover turned up, complete with Ted and Peter. By this time we were slowly crossing a piece of open plough. Ted turned the Rover round, ready to back up to the ditch. But this was not necessary at all. One could almost say that with a shout of joy Bear suddenly saw the car and started trundling in that direction. Tired she might be, but there was not even time to take the tailboard down. With a mighty heave she was in, and with one turn around, down she flounced, and sat there regarding us mere road creatures with the satisfied condescension of Queen Victoria, whom she sometimes much resembled. I am told that the ride home was uneventful, with Bear sitting in the back in state. But before the car had properly stopped in the yard, she had hurled herself out and had bundled back into her cage.

An amusing tailpiece to this adventure was the account of the telephone call from the luckless motorist, whom I had stopped. He appears to have carried out my request with a good deal of hesitation, which is not altogether surprising.

'Now I'm not drunk,' they tell me he began, 'but there's a young lady just stopped me, up on the airfield, who says her bear is exhausted——' Here the whole thing became too much for him and his voice trailed away. But I can just imagine his relief when whoever answered the telephone accepted this statement as a perfectly normal message. I am very much indebted to this kind motorist, and hope he enjoyed recounting a very comical incident.

15

More Walks

More than ever, now that Bear had become so enormous, the walk was the main theme of her life. What few people understood was the fascination of taking her for these walks. You take a dog; so you take a dog: very little out of the ordinary will happen—probably the highlight of the exercise will be when your supposedly perfect gundog destroys a nest of partridges.

But with Bear things were always happening: with her one entered a looking-glass world of discovery. And she reacted—my goodness how she reacted—not to mention the fact that one was always wondering *how* she would react. For instance, when I had to wallop all three labradors for chasing young pheasants, Bear was just curious to know what was happening, and why; but when Barney, a black and white mongrel with which I was landed, was unwise enough to attack Bruce in the middle of a cornfield, Bear became very agitated over the ensuing shindy, bouncing up and down and uttering mournful cries, much like an agitated Nannie who finds her children squabbling.

Another time, we suddenly came upon a clutch of young bullocks for the first time during a walk, and Bear was utterly unhinged. At first she hid behind my legs, peering out blindly at the strange white faces. Then she must have said to herself: 'This will never do. I really must try to be a little braver.' So, weaving out from behind me, she rushed at the bullocks—but not too close—and shouted 'Ho!' She rather cared for this form of attack and repeated it. The bullocks looked at her pityingly. 'Silly sort of dog,' they seemed to be saying among themselves. 'Ineffectual.' Perhaps Bear heard them, because she suddenly stood up and advanced on them in that terrifying way of hers.

They then hastily withdrew, and Bear, pride restored, was soon bored with the game, and wandered off on another tack.

Of course Bear's great objective during the summer months was digging out ants' nests; and when Bear dug, she dug: and there was a great deal of 'oo-er-ing' when it came to finding me again. But since these were not really her kind of ants, she made an enormous fuss when they crawled over her face and into her eyes. One remedy she had for this was to come up very quietly behind me and rub her head gently against my legs. As I nearly always wore slacks, the ants soon fell off me and it didn't worry me much. One day, though, I was not wearing slacks. I had come back from London, and thought if I did not waste time in changing, I would just have time to take Bear for a walk. It was a warm evening and I was wearing a wool jersey dress with a full skirt, and as it was quite dry I did not even bother to change my shoes. After Bear had had her usual settle-down gallop she came to walk behind me. It was then she must have noticed my different way of dress, for I felt a thoughtful snuffle at my nylons, and then a very peculiar sensation as she picked up the hem of my dress and carried it along in her mouth for all the world like a well-organised bridesmaid. It must have been the funniest thing to see, and a pity that there was no one with a camera standing by.

But suddenly she dropped my dress and started to make what I called her 'uneasy' noises—these were a sort of groan, such as you might expect if she had a tummy-ache. But when it was not a tummy-ache, it was because she had heard something disturbing through those hypersensitive great ears of hers. I looked around, wondering what it could be, but saw nothing and nobody around. We walked on, and the groans continued. But it was not until some ten minutes later, that I found what was disturbing her: there were several men from the farm putting up a large pheasant pen close by one of the spinneys, and she must have heard their voices all that way away.

To get to the pheasant pen we had to cross a small bridge over a stream and climb a narrow path through rough woodland. Bear galloped ahead to take a look at her men, most of whom nipped smartly inside the pen and closed the gate. But Ted, our gamekeeper, was left outside. I don't think Ted cared much for Bear, but he stood his ground while she reared up and said 'Ho!' at him.

'Oh, get down, Bear!' I said. 'We've had enough "Ho's" for today.' So as usual, with perfect docility, she got down, then, not finding the setting of the pheasant pen very attractive, I said goodbye to Ted, and turned to go back down the path again. It was a case of 'when father says turn we all turn' as there were eight dogs behind me in single file. There was Barney the mongrel in the lead, followed by the whippet, then the St Bernard with his shadow, the Welsh collie, then the three labradors and lastly the pekingese.

'Come along, Bear,' I called and started off. Suddenly there was a great 'whoosh' behind me, and I leapt to one side: on a very narrow path Bear definitely won on weight. She went charging past me, Pekie was knocked for six, the labradors scattered, she went over the Welsh collie and struck Louis, the enormous St Bernard, head-on from behind, just as he was crossing the bridge, and catapulted him into the stream. I really had to laugh at this avalanche act, and thought how slow the dogs were not to get out of her way. Not that she did it to hurt or annoy them—she was devoted to any dog that had once been walking with her—in fact she was a great deal nicer to them than they were to her. Barney and the collie and the whippet all used to snap at her when she first came out of her cage, but she made no effort to defend herself.

When the dogs had assembled again, we continued walking through the spinney and once more out into the open. It had been hot in the woods, and I had taken off my cardigan. Suddenly I felt it tweaked out of my hand, and there was Bear galloping across the field with it in her mouth, waving it joyfully from side to side. I wasn't at all pleased, and ran after her to rescue it. She thought this great fun, looked round briefly, and promptly turned a somersault as she trod on the trailing cardigan. I grabbed one end of it, she grabbed the other—the cardigan now forms part of the bush-baby's bed.

But Bear was really in a mood that day—a mood of enthusiasm and gaiety, that is to say. Bereft of the cardigan, she charged off towards a bank of high bracken, into which she disappeared. The rest of us started for home. In that bracken Bear must have found something exceedingly delectable, because the rest of us had gone right along the stream, crossed another bridge, and were well on our way before Bear's well-known cry was heard. This time I thought I would see just what she would do if I didn't call back, and if, without help, she would find us in the end. So I hung on to a willow branch and leant across the stream to watch her. She galloped this way and that, 'oo-er-ing' miserably and demonstrating pretty clearly that she had no scenting powers, for any dog would have picked up our trail at once. Much to my surprise she started to gallop right away from us, up the hill in the opposite direction. This was a bore, as, once outside the range of my considerable voice, there would be no way of getting her back except tagging after her, and we had been right round the farm already. So I let out a yell. Oh, what joy that unmusical sound was to her! Round she swung, and down the hill she came pelting, and I must say that for so oddly formed a creature, she was a jolly good mover downhill. Only once more I had to call her before she came panting up, quite exhausted, and I stroked her broad flat head.

'Why can't you smell,' I said. 'It's a terrible terrible thing to be a bear!'

'Pouf-pouf,' she panted back, and I wondered uneasily if all that galloping was very good for her. Poor Bear!

In many ways my ninth dog, I have walked miles with her. On any evening with the sun perhaps quite low in the sky, there we were, in our strange cavalcade, crossing the rolling fields, inspecting the hedges, discussing the merits of playing with the stick I nearly always carried. Sometimes we sat and Bear sat too. Close beside me, perhaps on top of me, while I ruffled the dull black shaggy coat and thought of the days when she was so small, so pathetic and when she roamed the house, as a cub. She remembered this, too. Not long ago she got in, rather by mistake, and wandered round looking and huffing. She remembered, I know she remembered, but I wonder what she made of the Christmas tree in the hall.

And then, after all those wonderful times together, one Sunday morning disaster struck. Bear attacked me savagely, and had to be destroyed.

So lie the bare bones of the story—but how much more is involved! Heartbreak once again, of course, at the loss of an animal I so dearly loved, and one who had a very special place in my heart, perhaps because of her lonely strangeness.

Informed Authority says (as well as the inevitable 'I told you so!') that I am in no way to blame. But this is naught for my comfort because I strongly disagree. I think I am very much to blame, for a number of reasons, but they all boil down to a hopeless lack of knowledge of all but the very simplest workings of the animal mind.

Bear had attacked me six weeks previously, in exactly the same manner. By chance my doctor, Basil Wilson Kaye, was with me—indeed, I had taken him out especially to look at Bear. It was a pretty hefty wound, but we got Bear back into her cage, he sewed me up without too much fuss, and that was that, for the time being. During that time Bear and I had other long happy walks together, but alone.

Where I went wrong, I think, was in putting this unheard of incident down to food frustration, when in fact it must have been pure jealousy. Perhaps, indeed, she had just attained sexual maturity, for her next, and fatal, attack on me was in precisely the same manner: a smell or a sight of a strange young man, at whom she promptly took a swipe, and when I corrected her, she administered a very bloody reprimand to me. What I shall never know is why these two men caused her such vicious jealousy, or why the person she loved best in the world, and trusted completely, luckily took the brunt of her displeasure. I only know that I failed her, because I did not know.

Well, now she lies buried by one of her favourite walks, in the home that she loved so well. And that is as it should be, because she had grown a long way beyond my very limited knowledge of a bear's mentality, yet never could I have condemned her to twenty or thirty years of dull, if not frightening captivity, after her gay life of freedom. Of all the animals I have ever owned she was the happiest, the sweetest tempered and the easiest to please. Of course she was as obstinate as an early martyr, as wayward as a delinquent teenager and as quick in movement as a humming bird—but she was always fun. Someday, somewhere, I should like to have world enough and time enough to study seriously the workings of the brilliant mind of a Sloth (or Beck's) Bear and to get to understand more clearly its highly developed instincts. In the meantime, if you are told, as you will be, that bears are utterly unpredictable, don't you believe it. It is only, as Joy Adamson would say, that *Homo sapiens* has not yet learned to predict.